The
Holiday Naturalist
in

FRANCE

Christopher O'Toole and Linda Losito

Illustrations by Paula Chasty

THE STEPHEN GREENE PRESS
Lexington, Massachusetts

OTHER BOOKS IN THE HOLIDAY NATURALIST SERIES

First published in Great Britain in 1987
by Christopher Helm Publishers Ltd
First published in the USA in 1987
by The Stephen Greene Press, Inc.
Published simultaneously in Canada
by Penguin Books Canada Ltd
Distributed by Viking Penguin Inc.,
40 West 23rd Street, New York, NY 10010.

CIP DATA available

ISBN 0-8289-0624-6
Produced for Christopher Helm Publishers Ltd by
Curtis Garratt Limited, The Old Vicarage,
Horton cum Studley, Oxford OX9 1BT

Map by Taurus Graphics
Photographic acknowledgements:
Title page Schlegelmilch/PRISMA: Planet Earth Pictures; *page 6* Richard
Packwood/Oxford Scientific Films; *page 11* G I Bernard/Oxford Scientific
Films; *page 14* Nickel/PRISMA: Planet Earth Pictures.

Filmset by SX Composing Ltd
Printed and bound in Hong Kong
by Mandarin Offset

Title page
Wild mountainous scenery from the Massif de la Vanoise in the central Savoy

CONTENTS

INTRODUCING FRANCE

France is the largest country in Western Europe. With an area of almost 200 000 square miles (500 000 square kilometres), it straddles a diverse range of impressive scenery and wildlife habitats. These range from the lowlands and chalk hills of the north, the French Alps in the east, to the sun-baked marshes, hillsides, and mountains of the Mediterranean south, the *Midi*. This variety of landform is matched by the climate and, together, they support a wealth of plant and animal life.

The lie of the land

The coastline of France is 1920 miles (3100 kilometres) long, and the country is bordered by three seas. France is also a land of broad, stately rivers. To the north, the Seine flows into the English Channel. The west coast confronts the Atlantic in all its moods; here the waters of the Garonne and France's longest river, the Loire, empty. In the south, the coast is lapped and warmed by the Mediterranean. And here, the waters of the Rhône meander and lose themselves in a delta of lagoons and marshes, where Flamingos and Bee-eaters vie with wild horses for the visitor's attention.

A line drawn from Mézières in the north-east, to Bayonne, in the south-west, conveniently divides France into two halves. For the most part, the north-western half comprises lowlands, and includes the massive Paris Basin, the plains of Brittany and Normandy and their rich, fertile farmlands. A low, eroded upland block (massif) of granite occupies the Brittany Peninsula and part of Normandy.

The south-western part is composed mainly of upland areas. Bordering Belgium and Luxembourg, the rounded, wooded hills of the Ardennes rise to heights of between 600 and 1600 feet (180 and 500 metres). Further east, along the border with Germany, the peaks of the Vosges range from 3000 to 5000 feet (900 to 1500 metres).

The Massif Central runs south from the centre of the country. It is France's most extensive upland region and occupies nearly one-sixth of its total area. The highest peak of the region is the Puy de Sancy, which reaches 6204 feet (1886 metres). The Massif is a huge, block-faulted plateau and, like the Ardennes and Vosges, owes its origin to the earliest period of mountain building in France. These earth movements took place towards the end of the Palaeozoic era, between 270 and 225 million years ago.

The southern part of the Massif Central embraces the Cevennes, a wild area of granite mountains and limestone plateaus. The latter, called *causses*, have a rich and distinctive flora and are dissected by deep gorges.

In the south-west, the Pyrénées form a continuous natural border with Spain and have peaks reaching 11 500 feet (3500 metres). The French Alps, bordering Switzerland, boast Europe's highest mountain, Mont Blanc, which towers 15 781 feet (4810 metres) above sea-level. The glaciated Pyrénées, Alps, and Jura are all recent mountain ranges. They are the wrinkles on the Earth's crust caused by the collision of the African continent with that of Europe resulting from continental drift. This mountain building started in the Triassic period, between 225 and 180 million years ago, but reached its most intense phase in the late Oligocene and Miocene, between twenty-eight and fifteen million years ago. It was also responsible for volcanic activity in the Auvergne region of the Massif Central, where the cones of extinct volcanoes form a major feature of the landscape.

Politically, the island of Corsica is part of France and lies some 100 miles (160 kilometres) from the coast of Provence. It is only 50

Standing at more than 5500 feet (1694 metres) is the peak of Puy Griou in the Massif Central.

miles (82 kilometres) from the coast of Italy, and the Corsican dialect is closer to Italian than it is to modern spoken French. Corsica is a large, mountainous island, with an area of 3365 square miles (8680 square kilometres), and is separated from Sardinia, its Italian neighbour to the south, by only 7½ miles (12 kilometres) of sea. Both islands were once part of what is now southern France; they broke away and began their southerly drift some time during the Tertiary, between 65 and 2.8 million years ago.

In more recent times, two important influences shaped the visual impact of modern French landscapes. First, almost all of the country escaped the effects of Ice Age glaciation. The contours of the land were gentled by time and the elements. Only the jagged peaks of the Jura, Alps, and Pyrénées suffered the gouging and scouring of glacial action.

The second major shaping force was human, with a polished stone axe. Neolithic man and his immediate descendants began to clear the natural, climax forest of oak, elm, and lime which covered all of lowland France. This process started about 5000 years ago and continued down the millennia. Nowadays, although forests make up a major landscape feature and, indeed, occupy about one-fifth of the land, the original climax forest of France has gone.

The climate

North and west-central France have a typical oceanic climate. That is, the pattern of winds, rainfall, and temperature changes is directly influenced by the Atlantic. The prevailing westerlies carry, on average, 100 depressions a year into western Europe, ensuring a steady flow of mild, damp air. The summers are warm, the winters mild, with most rain falling in autumn and winter. This means that there is only a small average temperature difference between summer and winter in western Europe – less than 20.7°F (11.5°C).

Eastern-central France, in contrast, has a continental climate. Here, the direct effects of the Atlantic are minimized by distance, and the East European high-pressure zone is the main influence. The summers are much warmer and the winters much colder, with many crisp, cloudless days. There is more summer rain, and the average temperature difference between summer and winter is greater – about 27°F (15°C).

The southern quarter of France has a Mediterranean climate, the most clear-cut of all European weather systems. The winters are mild, the summers very hot and dry. Rain falls throughout autumn, winter, and early spring, but it is irregular and occurs in short, heavy storms. This is the result of Atlantic depressions penetrating the western Mediterranean. In the summer, Atlantic depressions are deflected by subtropical high pressure from the Azores, and there is virtually no rain.

Strong winds of two types are characteristic of southern France. The *mistral* is a cold wind from the north and is particularly strong in the Rhône Valley in spring and autumn. It blows, on average, for 103 days of the year. In contrast, the *sirocco* can be hot and dry or warm and moist; it blows from North Africa on average for fifty days of the year.

Weather statistics for five French cities

	Average temperatures °F (°C)		Average annual rainfall in (mm)
	January	July	
Paris	38.3 (3.5)	64.4 (18)	23.9 (607)
Brest	45.5 (7.5)	62.6 (17)	33.1 (842)
Marseilles	44.1 (6.7)	72 (22.2)	22.6 (574)
Nice	43.7 (6.5)	70.3 (21.3)	31.7 (805)
Ajaccio (Corsica)	47.3 (8.5)	74.3 (23.5)	27.5 (698)

Artificial and seminatural habitats

General
With the loss of the original forests of France, most truly natural habitats went too. The main animal casualties were large species, such as the Wolf and Brown Bear, which competed with humans or were thought to do so. A combination of hunting and habitat destruction brought them to extinction. But the clearance of forest was gradual and, in its wake, new habitats were created, all more-or-less associated with human activities. Wild flowers and animals, which normally lived in woodland clearings and edges, colonized the new, marginal land. Plants adapted for life in disturbed ground, such as screes, land slips, or dry river beds, also gained a foothold in the newly developed farmland: poppies, Wild Chicory, and Cornflowers became the weeds of cultivated ground. In other words, the process of change during and after the first clearances was gradual enough to enable wildlife to respond and to adapt to new habitats which were roughly equivalent to original, natural ones. Human impact on the environment was, therefore, not entirely negative.

Nowadays, the waysides and hedgerows of France are a naturalist's delight. This is particularly true of the landscape pattern of the northern half of the country. The patchwork of small fields and clumps of woodland is called *bocage*. Far from being a system of windbreaks, as is often wrongly believed, it is a pattern of property boundaries. So far as the wildlife is concerned, the hedges function as corridors for the spread of woodland species from wood to wood, as well as havens in their own right for flowers, birds, and insects. The hay meadows they enclose are rich in flowers and butterflies, especially in chalky districts.

A noticeable feature of France is that not all agricultural land is under intensive use. In fact, at any one time, a third of the arable land lies fallow and may be abandoned for long periods. This encourages the development of scrub, providing habitats for wildlife.

Other artificial habitats are rich in wild flowers, birds, and insects. Old quarries abound in weedy annuals and often provide a home for crag-nesting birds of prey; disused sandpits attract Sand Martins and a host of wild wasps and bees, both of which excavate nests in sandy banks.

The wanderer through abandoned vineyard terraces and old Olive groves in the south will see (and hear) a rich insect life of crickets, grasshoppers, and cicadas. An electric blue-black flash here and there betrays the presence of Violet Carpenter Bees flitting from flower to flower. The occasional snake will make a sinuous retreat, and the slithering of lizards is everywhere. Overhead, there will be Bee-eaters and shrikes and, higher still, Buzzards riding high on thermals.

Finally, the visitor will notice another aspect of France which has a bearing on wildlife: with slightly more than fifty-four million people, France is a comparatively thinly populated country. The population density is an average of only 260 persons per square mile (100 persons per square kilometre); in Britain, for example, it is 570 persons per square mile (220 people per square kilometre).

Woodland

Forests occupy one-fifth of France's total area and comprise an important landscape feature providing many habitats for wildlife. Although the original climax forest has gone, many of the existing woodlands are very old and all have been managed, sometimes for centuries, either as a source of timber or as game and hunting reserves. France has perhaps the oldest tradition of forestry in Europe and her forests are well maintained by both state and private enterprises.

French forests support herds of deer, and Wild Boar is to be found still in the Vosges and Pyrénées. Dead and dying timber provide home and food for many insects and their predators. Woodland glades, rides, and edges are important for many wildflowers, birds, and butterflies. A stroll through a French forest glade on a spring day can be a rewarding experience: a profusion of flowers, the mellow fluting calls of Golden Orioles, and the distant hammering of woodpeckers.

Justly famous are the oak forests of Tronçais, Berce, and Reno-Valdieu in central France. The Forest of Fontainebleau, near Paris, is primarily of oak, while the classic beechwoods of France are centred at Lyons-la-Forêt. To the east, the Vosges boast dense forests of Beech, pine, and Silver Fir.

Spruce is the dominant forest tree on the higher parts of the French Alps. At lower altitudes, Spruce is found with patches of pines, Beech, and Birch. In the Jura, forests of oak, Ash, Beech, Hornbeam, and Sycamore are interspersed with woods of Pubescent Oak and Viburnum-leaved Maple, the last two species present because of the beginning of a Mediterranean influence. In the Pyrénées, the lower slopes are densely wooded with Beech which gives way to Silver Fir at higher altitudes, where it is dominant between 2500 and 4250 feet (750 and 1300 metres).

The Mediterranean south
For many holidaymakers, the *Midi*, with its hot summers and fine beaches, is the main attraction in France. But the south is also a paradise for those with an interest in natural history. After a few days of sand and sun, the visitor may wish to look inland and explore.

Around the coastal fringes, in isolated or protected areas, or in steep gorges running down to the sea, there are remnants of the original Mediterranean forest – a mixture of Cork Oak, Holm Oak, and the source of the edible pine kernel, the Aleppo Pine. The last species is often grown as an amenity tree in parks or in hillside plantations.

The dominant impression, however, is of dry, barren hillsides. A walk into the more remote inland areas may lead one to suppose that here, at least, we are dealing with the sort of natural habitat to be expected in an area of hot, dry summers. It looks right and it certainly smells right, with all the rich scents of Mediterranean cooking: growing all around are culinary herbs such as Thyme, Rosemary, Sage, Summer Savoury, Hyssop, and Rue. The scents of these herbs, which so endear them to cooks, are, in reality, a vital part of the survival kit for plants living in such arid conditions. The scented, essential oils evaporate very slowly and a cloud of tiny droplets is trapped by a dense clothing of pale or silvery hairs which covers the leaves and stems. This greatly reduces the loss of water vapour from the plant and helps to conserve a vital commodity in dry, well-drained soils, in a region so often buffeted by hot, desiccating winds.

Such close adaptations to the stresses of life in a Mediterranean climate, however, do not indicate that these are natural habitats. In fact, we are looking at the legacy of some 7000 to 8000 years of human interference and, in particular, the results of grazing by sheep and goats.

The shrubby and often spiny plant life of the Mediterranean hillsides is a combination of the kinds of plants which could withstand the rigours of the climate and millennia of grazing. Their natural habitats would have been in open areas and edges of Mediterranean forest and treeless rock faces.

Two kinds of vegetation replaced the original forests of the Mediterranean – *garrigue* and *maquis*. Typically, *garrigue* communities develop near the coast, often on very poor but well-drained chalky soils, where cultivation is impossible but grazing is practible. It is a rather open community of plants and it is in *garrigue* that the culinary herbs, already mentioned, come to the fore. The main flowering is in spring and there is usually a spectacular show of orchids, lilies, Wild Garlic, asphodel, and asphodelines. In fact, many of the spring-flowering bulbs loved by British gardeners originated in the Mediterranean *garrigue*.

A rich and diverse collection of wild bees is associated with *garrigue* and is conspicuous during the flowering season. This habitat favours many types of insects. Grasshoppers, crickets, and flower-visiting beetles abound, and female hunting wasps can be seen dragging their stung and paralyzed prey to their nests.

Garrigue is found all around the Mediterranean; in Spain it is called the *tomillares*, in Greece, *phrygana*, and it is known as *batha* in the countries of the eastern Mediterranean.

Maquis, in contrast, is a dense, almost impenetrable tangle of shrubs and low bushes, ranging in height from 6½ to 13 feet (2 to 4 metres). It gets its name as a corruption of the Corsican word *macchia*, for the Common Pink Rock-rose, which is one of the dominant shrubs of this community. This attractive plant exudes an aromatic gum called labdanum, which is used in medicinal plasters and in the perfume industry. Browsing goats accumulate large amounts of the gum on their beards as they pass by, and shepherds in many Mediterranean countries supplement their income by collecting it for sale. Tree Heather is another important *maquis* plant; its roots are of such dense, incombustible wood that they are used to make 'briar' pipes. Other important plants are Broom, Strawberry Tree, Juniper, and Myrtle.

Because of its dense cover, the *maquis* gave its name to the French Resistance of World War 2. It also provides plenty of cover for animals; tortoises can often be heard lumbering and munching there way through thickets of *maquis*. It forms a safe haven for small, migratory birds, as well as providing sheltered nest sites for resident species.

Whether it is the *bocage* of the north, the forests of the heartland, or the Mediterranean *maquis* and *garrigue*, the artificial habitats of France abound with a rich and varied wildlife. This testifies to the resilience of living things and the possibility that, with some exceptions, they can live in harmony with humans. Only in the twentieth century has the harmony come to be threatened by industrial pollution and intensive agriculture.

Natural habitats

The human appetite for land has meant that the relatively few natural habitats which remain in France are either difficult of access, such as high alpine areas, or remote rivers and lakes. Marginal habitats, too, such as salt and freshwater marshes and coastal sand-dunes, have survived in many places. Because they are natural habitats and therefore rare, they and their plants and animals are recognized as special and worthy of protection. We discuss them in the next section on national parks and nature reserves.

The dense tangle of shrubs and low bushes making up maquis *habitat from southern France.*

This leaves us with the two seas which have such an important influence on the climates of France, the Atlantic and the Mediterranean. Both are, of course, important habitats in their own right.

The coasts of western Europe are bathed in relatively warm waters brought from the tropical south by the North Atlantic Drift. The Atlantic coasts of France benefit from this and there are many coastal regions of interest to the holiday naturalist. The rocky coasts of Brittany and Normandy are rich in areas where intertidal rock pools are accessible, affording a fascinating glimpse into shallow-water marine life. After storms, many animals, such as the Spider Crab, normally denizens of deep water, are washed up and test our powers of identification.

Wide expanses of sandy beaches are well developed along the south-western coasts and are almost continuous from the mouth of the Gironde to the Spanish border. Here, the beaches are often backed by impressive dune systems and brackish-water lagoons. The dunes are particularly well developed in the Les Landes region, south of Bordeaux. Here, vast stands of pines have been planted to stabilize the windblown sand and to prevent its relentless landward march. The pines are extensively tapped for resin, which is distilled into turpentine.

The Mediterranean is an almost landlocked sea. It connects with the Atlantic by the narrow Straits of Gibraltar. The Straits themselves lie across a shallow shelf, so that the rate of water flow in and out of the Mediterranean is impeded and therefore slow. Inward flow is in the form of a shallow stream from the Atlantic, of rather cool water. The outward flow is of heavier water, which spills out over the Gibraltar sill. The water is heavier because the Mediterranean is saltier than the Atlantic, with 37 to 39 parts per thousand of salt, compared with the Atlantic's 35 parts per thousand. A high rate of evaporation – as high as 4 million cubic feet (115 000 cubic metres) per second – accounts for the high salinity. Also, the rivers flowing into the sea carry dissolved salts.

Broadly speaking, the waters of the Mediterranean flow in an anticlockwise direction and tidal fluctuations are small. The landlocked nature of the sea, the slow rate of interchange with the

11

Atlantic, and the reduced tidal scouring all conspire to make the Mediterranean very susceptible to pollution. The situation is not helped by the practice of discharging untreated industrial and domestic sewage into the sea by many countries bordering the Mediterranean.

Rock pools along the southern coast of France are well worth exploring because they harbour many kinds of animals, including corals, which are not found in the waters of the colder Atlantic.

National Parks and Nature Reserves
There are several categories of protected land in France. Of these, the six National Parks are the most important. Eighty-three per cent of these are in mountainous areas and 50 per cent of all protected areas are in the Alps.

National Parks
Each National Park is divided into an Inner or Central Zone and a Peripheral Zone. Wildlife preservation is the main objective in Central Zones. With few exceptions, hunting is prohibited. Road construction and building and industrial development are banned. Each Inner Zone is run by a director and his/her staff, with the help of a scientific committee and administrative council.

The Peripheral Zone is controlled by a Departmental Committee, and the main objective is to cater for the needs of tourists, while preserving traditional landscapes, architecture, and ways of life.

Regional Parks
Twenty-six Regional Parks were established under legislation passed in 1967. The objectives are similar to those of the Peripheral Zones of National Parks but additionally, they are designed to stimulate the local economy. Wildlife conservation has no special emphasis, and hunting is unrestricted except where there happens to be a Nature Reserve within a National Park.

State Nature Reserves
For a country of its size, France has relatively few State Nature Reserves. Three-hundred-and-fifty sites considered to be of national importance have been recognized and, in 1971, 100 were selected for preservation. Government policy, however, is to seek management agreements with private landowners and to avoid the outright purchase of land. Progress has been slow.

Private Reserves
Private nature conservation societies have been responsible for the creation of many important nature reserves. Most private reserves are in Brittany where the oldest conservation body in France, the Society for the Study and Protection of Nature in Brittany, is active. The National Society for the Protection of Nature (SNPN) is the most effective nationally organized private body.

Other forms of wildlife protection
Although the hunting fraternity in France has often had a bad

press, its effects are not entirely negative. Many hunting associations have established game or hunting reserves. Although game, such as deer and Wild Boar, are shot, the preservation of whole habitats is beneficial to wildlife in general. In some game reserves, such as the Pointe d'Arsay, shooting is prohibited.

National Parks, Regional Parks, and Nature Reserves

National Parks
1 **Parc National de la Vanoise** *Situation* central Savoy Alps, between valleys of l'Arc and l'Isère, bordering Italy for 4¼ miles (7 kilometres) and Italy's major conservation area, the Gran Paradiso National Park. *Area* 204 square miles (528.4 square kilometres). *Special features* a high alpine region, 4100-12670 feet (1250-3852 metres); geology a complex mixture of crystalline and lime-rich rocks; extensive coniferous forests; varied plant life, including primulas, gentians, campanulas, and anemones; butterflies include Apollo, Scarce Copper, Mountain Clouded Yellow; other animals include Golden Eagle, Buzzard, Ptarmigan, Pine Marten, Ibex. *Information* Parc National de la Vanoise, 135 rue de Docteur Julliand, B.P.105, 73003 Chambery cedex. *Access* unrestricted.

2 **Parc National des Ecrins** *Situation* Departments of Isère and Hautes Alpes and Pelvaux Wildlife Reserve. *Area* 417 square miles (1080 square kilometres). *Special features* outstanding alpine scenery at altitudes between 2600 and 13500 feet (800 and 4102 metres), with glaciers, lakes, gorges, larch forests; includes six Nature Reserves; superb plant life, including Lady's Slipper Orchid; animals include Golden Eagle, Capercaillie, Ptarmigan, Mountain Hare and Fox, Chamois. *Information* Maison du Parc National des Ecrins, 05290, Vallouise. *Access* unrestricted.

3 **Parc National des Cévennes** Situation Departments of Lòzere, Gard and Ardèche, in southern Massif Central. *Special features* limestone plateaus with deep gorges, hills and mountains of crystalline rock from 4600-5600 feet (1400-1700 metres); extensive coniferous plantations, oak, Chestnut, and Beech forests; rich plant life, including more than forty orchid species, Wild Daffodils, and Tulips. Animals include Eagle Owl, Peregrine, Ortolan Buntings, Stone Curlew, Little Bustard, Hen and Montagu's Harriers. *Information* Parc National des Cévennes, Château de Florac, B.P. 4, 48400, Florac. *Access* unrestricted.

4 **Parc National du Mercantour** *Situation* between Alpes-Maritimes and Italian border, north of St-Martin-Vésubie. *Area* 270 square miles (700 square kilometres). *Special features* a diverse region of strongly eroded granite hills and mountains, with the richest plant life in France, combining alpine, central European, and Mediterranean elements; insect life very rich, with many kinds restricted to the area, including the Larch Ringlet and Small Apollo butterflies; mammals and birds include Ibex, Chamois, Golden Eagle, Eagle Owl, buzzards, Sparrowhawk, harriers, and kites.

Information Parc National du Mercantour, 13, rue Maccarani, 06000, Nice. *Access* unrestricted.

5 Parc National des Pyrénées Orientales *Situation* Department of Hautes-Pyrénées, south-west of Tarbes, near Spanish border. *Area* 177 square miles (457 square kilometres). *Special features* outstanding mountain scenery, at altitudes between 3300 and 11 000 feet (1000 and 3300 metres); extensive forests of mountain pine and beech, with varied plant life, including many restricted species. Animals include Brown Bear, Genet, Martens, Foxes, Badgers, Chamois. *Information* Parc National des Pyrénées Occidentales, route de Pau, B.P. 300, 65013, Tarbes. *Access* unrestricted.

6 Parc National de Port-Cros *Situation* Mediterranean island 6 miles (10 kilometres) south of Côte d'Azure, reached by boat from La Lavandou. *Area* 6 square miles (15.9 square kilometres). *Special features* more than half of this National Park is under water, to protect its rich marine life, including eels, groupers, and marine plants; land plants include good examples of Mediterranean evergreen forest, Holm Oak, Aleppo Pine, as well as *maquis*. Insect life exceptionally rich, with 220 butterfly species, including the Two-tailed Pasha; also, 600 beetle species; few mammals, but several kinds of lizards and six types of snake; the island is an important refuge for migratory birds, and Cory's Shearwaters breed. *Information* Parc National de Port-Cros, 50, avenue Gambetta, 83400, Hyères. *Access* unrestricted, except for islet of Bagaud, which is closed to visitors.

Regional Parks
1 Parc d'Armorique *Situation* Department of Finistère. *Area* 330 square miles (850 square kilometres). *Special features* typical *bocage* landscape, heaths, moors, bogs; Common and Grey Seals, Fallow Deer, Wild Boar; moorland areas have interesting plants and insects. *Information* Maison du parc naturel régional d'Armorique, Menez-Meur, 29247, Hanvec. *Access* unrestricted.

The rocky coastline of Brittany offers the holiday naturalist a rich diversity of rock pools to explore.

2 **Parc de Brière** *Situation* Department of Loire-Atlantique. *Area* 155 square miles (400 square kilometres). *Special features* huge area of lagoons, marshes, and hay meadows, rich in wildfowl and marsh plants. *Information* Maison du parc naturel régional de Brière, 180, Ile de Fédrun, 44720 St Joachim. *Access* unrestricted.

3 **Parc des Vosges du Nord** *Situation* Departments of Bas-Rhin, Moselle. *Area* 42½ square miles (110 square kilometres). *Special features* oak and Beech woods, peat bogs, limestone grassland, rich fossil beds in lime-rich rocks, with special 'geological walks' laid out in parts. *Information* Maison du parc régional des Vosges du Nord, La Petite-Pierre, 67290, Wingen-sur-Moder. *Access* unrestricted.

4 **Parc des Volcans d'Auvergne.** *Situation* Departments of Puy-de-Dôme, Cantal. *Area* 1087 square miles (2815 square kilometres). *Special features* spectacular scenery of volcanic cones, some containing lakes; forests of oak, Sweet Chestnut, beech and firs; rich plant life including White Narcissus, Yellow Gentian, swards of violets; fine bird life, including Short-toed Eagle, Goshawk, Red Kite, Buzzard. *Information* Maison du parc naturel régional des Volcans d'Auvergne, château de Montlosier, Randanne, 63210, Rochefort-Montagne. *Access* unrestricted.

5 **Parc du Pilat** *Situation* Department of Loire. *Area* 232 square miles (600 square kilometres). *Special features* wooded hills, with Poplar, Downy Oak, and Sweet Chestnut between 1300 and 2600 feet (400 and 800 metres), with pine, beech, and fir on higher slopes; interesting mountain plants and birds including Bonelli's Eagle and Crag Martins; ideal area to watch autumn migrants flying south; Red and Roe Deer, Wild Boar. *Information* Maison du parc naturel régional du Pilat, Le moulin de Vireu, 2 rue Benäy, 42410, Pelussin. *Access* unrestricted.

6 **Parc du Vercors** *Situation* Departments of Isère, Drôme. *Area* 521 square miles (1350 square kilometres). *Special features* subalpine plateau, with average altitude of 4000 feet (1200 metres); spectacular cliffs and gorges, rich mountain pasture, with gentians and many types of orchid; pines, spruce, beech on north-facing slopes, Scots Pine and Downy Oak on southern slopes; Red and Roe Deer, Wild Boar. *Information* Maison du parc naturel régional du Vercors, Chemin des Fusillés, B.P. 14, 38250 Lansen-Vercors. *Access* unrestricted.

7 **Parc du Lubéron** *Situation* Departments of Vaucluse, Alpes de Haute-Provence. *Area* 464 square miles (1200 square kilometres). *Special features* mountain ridge with extensive and largely coppiced oak forest, *maquis* and about 2500 acres (1000 hectares) of Atlas Cedars planted in 1860; noted caves and typical rural landscape of Provence; rare birds include Egyptian Vulture, Short-toed Eagle, and Bonelli's Eagle. *Information* Maison du parc

naturel régional du Lubéron, avenue des Druides, 84400 Apt. *Access* unrestricted.

8 **Parc de la Camargue** (Regional Park and Nature Reserve) *Situation* Department Bouches-du-Rhône. *Area* 367 square miles (951.2 square kilometres). *Special features* delta of River Rhône, with internationally important wetlands, including brackish lakes, salt steppe, and salt marshes, with dunes and riverine forest; many rare birds, including Flamingo, Bittern, Little Bittern, Squacco Heron, Night Heron, Purple Heron, Rollers, Great Spotted Cuckoo; Bee-eaters breed on the reserve; rich insect life, and specialized sand-dune animals such as solitary wasps and bees. *Information* Parc naturel régional de Camargue, Le Mas du Pont-de-Rousty, 13200 Arles. *Access* unrestricted.

9 **Parc de la Corse** *Situation* Corsica. *Area* 579 square miles (1500 square kilometres). *Special features* outstanding mountain scenery, with twenty granitic peaks exceeding 6600 feet (2000 metres); fifty-eight plant species restricted to the area, that is, 8 per cent of the total plant life; extensive pine forests; Cork and Holm Oaks; good *maquis*, with Tree Heather, Myrtle, Vibernum, and Strawberry Tree; excellent bird life, including Lammergeier, Osprey, Cory's Shearwater, Goshawk, Red Kite, Bee-eater, Alpine Accentor, and Blue Rock Thrush; very rich insect life. *Information* Maison du parc naturel régional de Corse, Palaise Lantivy, B.P. 147, 20184 Ajaccio cedex. *Access* unrestricted.

Nature Reserves
1 **Cap Frehel** *Situation* promontory between St Malo and St Brieuc, Brittany. *Area* 1½ square miles (4 square kilometres). *Special features* rocky cliffs with many nesting seabirds, including Herring Gulls, Shag, Puffin, Fulmar, and Kittiwake, and Raven; grass-topped promontory with Wild Daffodils, Solomon's-seal, Bluebells. *Information* Société pour l'étude et la protection de la nature en Bretagne, Faculté des Sciences, avenue Le Gorgeu, 29200, Brest. *Access* unrestricted.

2 **Marquenterre** *Situation* mouth of the River Somme. *Area* 9 square miles (23 square kilometres). *Special features* vast area of saltmarsh and dunes, rich in wildfowl and waders; breeding species include Shelduck, Little Grebe, Oystercatcher, Greylag Goose, Kentish Plover, and Avocet. *Information* Parc ornithologique du Marquenterre, St Quentin-en-Tourmont, 80120 Rue. *Access* 1 April-4 November, between 9.30 am and 6.00 pm.

3 **Vallée de La Grande Pierre et de Vitain** *Situation* Loire Valley, 5 miles (8 kilometres) north of Blois. *Area* 1¼ square miles (2.96 square kilometres). *Special features* hard limestone area in valley of the River Cisse; rich in lime-loving plants, including Lizard Orchid; undisturbed limestone grassland with interesting invertebrate life. *Information* Office de Tourisme, Pavillon Anne de Bretagne, 3 avenue Jean-Laigret, 41000 Blois. *Access* unrestricted.

HOW TO USE THIS BOOK

The colour plates are arranged according to groups; for example, mammals, birds, and so on but, for ease of reference, the section on plants is arranged by flower colour.

This is not intended to be an exhaustive or comprehensive identification guide. Instead, we have selected plants and animals on the basis of those which the holidaymaker is likely to see. Our aim is to give a good idea of the commonest kinds of animals and plants, without the threat to baggage allowances posed by a set of more comprehensive field guides. If our book stimulates a special interest in any particular group of animals or plants, then the holidaymaker can explore this in more detail using one or more of the guides listed under 'Further reading'.

Key to the habitat symbols

 coniferous and deciduous woodlands and forests

 heaths, moors, and dry grasslands

 marshes, swamps, and damp meadows

 inland fresh water: rivers, streams, ponds, lakes, etc

 uplands: hills and mountains

 coastal: dunes, saltings, seacliffs, estuaries, sea

 farmland and marginal areas

 parks, gardens, urban areas

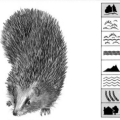

Hedgehog. *Length* 8¾-10½ in (22-27 cm). *Call* an occasional shrill whistle; also sighs, grunts, and snuffles. *Habitat* open woodland, hedgerows, gardens, usually at dusk. Hibernates among dead vegetation.

Rabbit *Length* 14-17½ in (35-45 cm). *Colour* occasionally black. *Habitat* woodland, grassy meadows, cultivated fields; form colonies in underground burrows; most active at dusk and early morning.

Brown Hare *Length* 19-25½ in (48-65 cm). *Call* occasional grunts and whistles. *Habitat* scrubby woodland, open fields, and farmland; nest above ground, solitary; largely nocturnal except during courtship.

Red Squirrel *Length* body 7½-11 in (19-28 cm), tail 5½-10 in (14-24 cm). *Colour* changes from pale red to dark brown in winter; ears develop tufts of hair. *Call* a harsh 'tjuk-tjuk-tjuk'. *Habitat* pine or beech woodland, parks.

Common Weasel *Length* body 6¼-9 in (16-23 cm), tail 1½-2½ in (4-6 cm); females much smaller than males. *Call* a shrill whistle. *Habitat* woodland, scrub, in low-lying or more mountainous regions; largely nocturnal.

Stoat or Ermine *Length* body 8¾-11½ in (22-29 cm), tail 3-4¾ in (8-12 cm). *Colour* winter form white in some areas; unlike smaller Weasel, has black tail tip. *Call* a repetitive, high-pitched 'kree-kree'. *Habitat* damp woodland; largely nocturnal.

Common Vole *Length* body 4-4¾ in (10-12 cm), tail 1¼-1½ in (3-4 cm). *Call* short, high-pitched squeak. *Habitat* grassy fields and meadows; tunnels underground; partly nocturnal.

Dormouse *Length* body 2½-3½ in (6-9 cm), tail 2-2¾ in (5-7 cm). *Call* series of soft whistles, clicks, and growls. *Habitat* woodland, hedgerows, parks; very agile climbers; nest in treeholes or among branches; nocturnal.

European Polecat *Length* body 12½-17½ in (32-45 cm), tail 5-7½ in (13-19 cm); females smaller than males. *Call* growling and chattering when disturbed. *Habitat* forested areas; hunt mainly on the ground but will climb trees.

Stone or Beech Marten *Length* body 16½-19 in (42-48 cm), tail 9-10 in (23-26 cm). *Call* a loud 'tok-tok-tok', also growling and chattering. *Habitat* woodland edge in mountainous regions; will nest in outbuildings; nocturnal.

Pine Marten *Length* body 16½-20½ in (42-52 cm), tail 8¾-10 in (22-26 cm). *Call* 'tok-tok-tok', also growls, chatters, and wails. *Colour* distinguished from Beech Marten by yellow throat. *Habitat* coniferous woodland; active climber; partly nocturnal.

Red Fox *Length* body 23-30 in (58-77 cm), tail 12½-19 in (32-48 cm). *Call* a range of barks, whimpers, and screams. *Colour* occasional black or white forms occur. *Habitat* woodland, scrub, and in towns; largely nocturnal.

Muskrat *Length* body 10-15½ in (26-40 cm), tail 7½-10½ in (19-27 cm). *Call* occasional whistle. *Habitat* riverbanks, ponds, streams, where vegetation is dense; builds a 'house' of branches and reeds in winter.

Wild Cat *Length* body 20-31½ in (50-80 cm), tail 11-14 in (28-35 cm). *Call* loud wails and miaows. *Colour* some dark forms exist. *Habitat* scrubby hillsides and woodland; nocturnal.

Wild Boar *Length* body 35½-70 in (90-180 cm), tail 6-8 in (15-20 cm). *Call* chatters, barks, and snorts. *Habitat* broadleaved woodland; often wallow in muddy ponds; active during day and evening.

Roe Deer *Length* 37½-53 in (95-135 cm). *Height* at shoulder 25¼-35 in (64-89 cm). *Call* short barks, male calls deeper. *Colour* grey in winter, with conspicuous white areas on rump. *Habitat* forest edge, moorland, woodland.

Great Northern Diver *Length* 26¾-32 in (68-81 cm). *Call* 'kwuk-kwuk-kwuk' in flight, otherwise a loud wailing cry. *Habitat* winter visitor, frequenting coastal waters, usually in small parties.

Red-throated Diver *Length* 21-22¾ in (53-58 cm). *Call* a highly pitched 'kwuk-kwuk-kwuk' in flight, otherwise wailing or barking croak. *Habitat* coastal waters in winter, often in small flocks.

Great Crested Grebe *Length* 19 in (48 cm). *Call* a shrill 'er-wick' and a barking 'kar-arr'. *Habitat* freshwater lakes; colonial nesting in floating vegetation, wintering in estuaries and coastal waters; resident.

Fulmar *Length* 18½ in (47 cm). *Call* hoarse chuckling or grunting 'ag-ag-ag-arrr', heard mainly at breeding sites. *Habitat* winter resident along northern coast only; summer visitor around Finistère.

Manx Shearwater *Length* 13¾ in (35 cm). *Call* raucous crowing and crooning sounds, especially at night at breeding sites. *Habitat* open seas; winter visitor.

Gannet *Length* 35½ in (90 cm). *Call* a barking 'arrah'. *Habitat* open seas, winter visitor, making spectacular dives into water after fish, sometimes from heights of 100 ft (30 m) or more.

Shag *Length* 30 in (76 cm). *Call* loud hissing and deep grunts at nest, otherwise a loud rasping croak. *Habitat* strictly marine, nesting on rocky coasts, rarely visiting sandy or muddy shores or inland; resident breeder.

Cormorant *Length* 35½ in (90 cm). *Call* a low, deep 'r-rah'. *Habitat* coasts, estuaries, coastal lagoons, occasionally inland lakes; colonial nests on rock ledges, occasionally trees on inland lakes; resident breeder.

Grey Heron *Length* 35½ in (90 cm). *Call* a harsh 'frank'; in breeding season, retching and croaking noises. *Habitat* rivers, lakes, damp meadows, seashore, nesting colonially in tall trees; resident breeder in north, otherwise winter visitor.

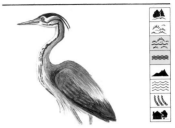

Purple Heron *Length* 31 in (79 cm). *Call* similar to that of Grey Heron, but usually less vocal. *Habitat* dense reedbeds, overgrown ditches and swamps, nesting colonially in reedbeds, sometimes in bushes; resident breeder.

Little Egret *Length* 22 in (56 cm). *Call* in breeding season, a croaking 'kark' and a bubbling 'wulla-wulla-wulla'. *Habitat* swamps, lagoons, and marshes; nesting in bushes, trees, sometimes woods; summers in south-east, winters in south-west.

Little Bittern *Length* 13¾ in (35 cm). *Call* short croaking notes or a song comprising deep croaks every two seconds, often for hours at a time. *Habitat* reedbeds, wooded swamps, ponds, overgrown rivers; resident, and breeds in summer.

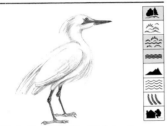

Bittern *Length* 30 in (76 cm). *Call* in flight, a harsh 'kwow', with a low, penetrating booming song carrying for distances of up to 1 mile (1.6 km). *Habitat* dense reedbeds in fens, marshes, and lakesides; breeding resident.

Spoonbill *Length* 34 in (86 cm). *Call* occasional grunting noises in breeding season; bill-clattering when excited. *Habitat* shallow, open water in reedy marshes or estuaries; regular spring/autumn migrant.

White Stork *Length* 40 in (102 cm). *Call* infrequent hissing and coughing notes; rhythmic bill-clattering during displays. *Habitat* farmland, damp meadows, marshes; spring/autumn migrant.

Great Flamingo *Length* 50 in (127 cm). *Call* a goose-like honking in flight, with a trumpeting 'ar-honk'. *Habitat* coastal lagoons, mudflats, lakes; conical mud nests in shallow water in Rhône Delta.

Mute Swan *Length* 59¾ in (152 cm). *Call* habitually silent but has occasional trumpeting note; hissing and snorting when annoyed. *Habitat* remote marshes and lakes in truly wild state, otherwise any freshwater lakes; breeding resident.

Greylag Goose *Length* 30-35 in (76-89 cm). *Call* a loud 'aahng-ung-ung' in flight, otherwise a reedy gabbling like the domestic goose, which is derived from Greylag. *Habitat* estuaries, grasslands near coasts; winter visitor.

Shelduck *Length* 24 in (61 cm). *Call* rarely vocal outside breeding season, otherwise a nasal 'ak-ak-ak' and a deeper 'ark, ark'. *Habitat* sandy and muddy coasts; breeds along north and south coasts, nesting in rabbit burrows.

Mallard *Length* 22¾ in (58 cm). *Call* female, a loud quacking, male a quiet 'yeeb'. *Habitat* almost any water, wintering sometimes on seacoasts and estuaries; resident breeder.

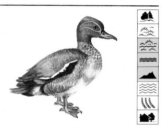

Teal *Length* 13¾ in (35 cm). *Call* female, a harsh quack, male a low, musical 'krrt'. *Habitat* reedy pools, wintering on marshes, sometimes on coastal waters and estuaries; resident breeder in north, otherwise a winter visitor.

Pintail *Length* 22 in (56 cm). *Call* female a low quack, and a growling note, male a low whistle, but both sexes rarely vocal. *Habitat* mainly a winter visitor, frequenting coastal waters; breeds irregularly on marshes, moors, sand-dunes.

Shoveler *Length* 20 in (51 cm). *Call* female a double quack, male a gruff 'took, took', flight call a deep 'tuk-tuk'. *Habitat* marshes, overgrown ponds; resident breeder, nesting in marshes and water-meadows.

Red-crested Pochard *Length* 22 in (56 cm). *Call* a grating 'kurr', usually in flight. *Habitat* large, usually reedy freshwater lakes, brackish lagoons, rarely on sea; resident breeder in south-west, nesting among vegetation on islands.

Common Scoter *Length* 19 in (48 cm). *Call* female, a harsh growl, male several melodious, cooing notes. *Habitat* coastal waters in winter.

Red-breasted Merganser *Length* 21-22¾ in (53-58 cm). *Call* usually silent, male with rasping courtship note, female a guttural 'karr'. *Habitat* winter resident on coastal waters, estuaries, rarely on inland fresh waters.

White-headed Duck *Length* 18 in (46 cm). *Call* usually silent, but drakes cluck and squeak in breeding season. *Habitat* shallow, reedy, freshwater and brackish pools; winter resident in south-east.

Osprey *Length* 20-22¾ in (51-58 cm). *Call* a shrill cheeping. *Habitat* moorland or wooded country with lakes and rivers, wintering near large expanses of fresh, brackish, or salt water; spring and autumn passage migrant.

Red Kite *Length* 24 in (61 cm). *Call* a high, buzzard-like mewing. *Habitat* wooded hills, open areas with scattered trees, sometimes seen feeding on animals killed by road traffic; summer visitor.

Black Kite *Length* 22 in (56 cm). *Call* high-pitched squealing cries, very noisy in breeding season. *Habitat* open woodland, scattered trees near lakes and rivers, sometimes in towns and villages; summer visitor.

Short-toed or Snake Eagle *Length* 24¾-27¼ in (63-69 cm). *Call* loud, either a harsh 'jee', a buzzard-like 'mew-ok' or a weak 'ok, ok, ok'. *Habitat* open country, with scattered woods; feeds mainly on snakes in south; breeding summer visitor.

Sparrowhawk *Length* 11-15 in (28-38 cm). *Call* chattering, based on 'kek', 'kew', 'kyow', or 'kiv'. *Habitat* woodland, farmland, coppices, nesting in fir trees in mixed woods; presence indicated by feathers, fur under perches; resident breeder.

Goshawk *Length* 19-24 in (48-61 cm). *Call* male, a shrill 'ca-ca-ca-ca' or 'qek-qek-qek-qek', from female a screaming 'hi-aa', 'hi-aa'. *Habitat* both broad-leaved and coniferous forests; resident breeder.

Buzzard *Length* 20-22 in (51-56 cm). *Call* sometimes a short, croaking note, or a long drawn-out, high mewing 'pee-oo'. *Habitat* forests and areas with scattered woods, rocky coasts; resident breeder, nests on rock ledges, trees.

Honey Buzzard *Length* 20-22¾ in (51-58 cm). *Call* a high, squeaky 'kee-er' and a rapid 'kikiki'. *Habitat* open glades and outskirts of deciduous woods; robs wasps' and bees' nests; breeding summer visitor, using old crows' nests.

Bonelli's Eagle *Length* 26-29 in (66-74 cm). *Call* a Goshawk-like chattering 'kie, kie, kikiki'. *Habitat* rocky mountains, wintering in plains; resident breeder in south, nesting on steep cliff faces, sometimes in trees.

Golden Eagle *Length* 29½-34½ in (75-88 cm). *Call* a few whistling notes, occasionally a yelping 'kya'. *Habitat* open mountain country, sometimes a mountain forest; resident breeder in Massif Central and south-east, nests on crags or in tree.

Spotted Eagle *Length* 26-29 in (66-74 cm). *Call* a dog-like yapping, 'kyak-kyak-kyak'. *Habitat* lowland forest, near lakes, rivers and marshes; in south-west only, a winter visitor.

Egyptian Vulture *Length* 22¾-26 in (58-66 cm). *Call* usually silent. *Habitat* open country in mountains and lowlands; breeding summer visitor in south, nest on cliffs, in trees.

Bearded Vulture or Lammergeier *Length* 40¼-44¾ in (102-114 cm). *Call* silent except in display, when a thin 'quee-er'. *Habitat* high, remote, rocky mountains; resident breeder in Pyrénées, Corsica, Sardinia, nests on rock ledges.

Griffon Vulture *Length* 38¼-41 in (97-104 cm). *Call* grunting and whistling noises in breeding season only. *Habitat* usually mountains, but wide ranging; resident breeder in Pyrénées, nests socially on rock ledges, in caves.

Marsh Harrier *Length* 19-22 in (48-56 cm). *Call* a high, Lapwing-like 'quee-a'. *Habitat* fens, swamps, marshes, and large reedbeds; resident breeder, large nest in reedbed, usually surrounded by water.

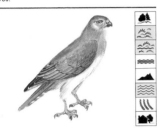

Hen Harrier *Length* 17-20 in (43-51 cm). *Call* a shrill, chattering 'ke-ke-ke', or a long, wailing 'pee-e'. *Habitat* moors, steppes, coastal dunes, marshes, reedbeds; winter visitor on north and south coasts, otherwise a resident breeder, nest on ground.

Montagu's Harrier *Length* 16-18 in (41-46 cm). *Call* 'kek-kek-kek', shriller than Hen Harrier. *Habitat* fens, marshes, farmland, moors with tree clumps; breeding summer visitor, nests on dry heaths, sociably in wet vegetation.

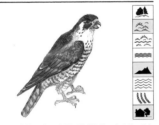

Peregrine Falcon *Length* 15-19 in (38-48 cm). *Call* mainly a harsh chattering note, wide range in breeding season, including 'we-chew', 'kek-kek-kek'. *Habitat* wild mountains, moors, spires; breeds on crags, cliffs.

Hobby *Length* 11¾-14 in (30-36 cm). *Call* a distinct 'ket' or 'kew', and a rapid 'kikikiki'. *Habitat* open woodland, grassy hills with scattered trees; resident breeder, breeds in trees, often in old crows' nests.

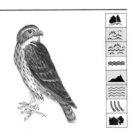

Merlin *Length* 10½-13 in (27-33 cm). *Call* male, a rapid, high-pitched 'ki-ki-ki-ki', female a lower chatter, with a slow 'eep-eep'. *Habitat* open hill country, wet moors, cliffs, and dunes; winter visitor.

Red-footed Falcon *Length* 11¾ in (30 cm). *Call* a shrill 'kikikiki', higher than Kestrel. *Habitat* open plains with scattered scrub, woodland edges and around farms; spring/autumn passage migrant.

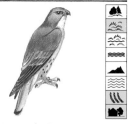

Lesser Kestrel *Length* 11¾ in (30 cm). *Call* a chattering 'chet', a plaintive 'whee'. *Habitat* hunts over open country, glides more than hovers; breeding summer visitor, breeds colonially on crags, old buildings.

Kestrel *Length* 13½ in (34 cm). *Call* usually silent outside breeding season; shrill, repeated 'kee, kee, kee' and a musical 'kee-lee'. *Habitat* open woodland, farmland with scattered trees; resident breeder, breeds in old crows' nests.

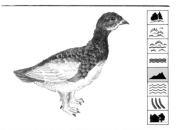

Ptarmigan *Length* 14 in (35-36 cm). *Call* a harsh croak, crackling note when alarmed, displaying males a brief, crowing 'song'. *Habitat* high, bare mountain slopes; resident breeder in Massif Central, Pyrénées, nest on ground.

Capercaillie *Length* 24½ in (62 cm). *Call* male an accelerating 'tik-up, tik-up, tik-up', ending with loud 'pop', a retching call in display, female a Pheasant-like 'kok-kok'. *Habitat* hilly, coniferous forests; nests on ground in uplands.

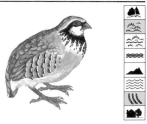

Red-legged Partridge *Length* 13½ in (34 cm). *Call* male, 'chuck', 'chuck-er', or a slow, harsh 'tschreck, tschreck', 'kuk-kuk' when disturbed. *Habitat* fields, moors, dry hillsides; breeding resident, nests on ground, well hidden.

Partridge *Length* 11¾ in (30 cm). *Call* a loud, grating 'krr-ic', a rapidly repeated 'kar-wic' when excited. *Habitat* moors, fields, farmland, dunes; resident breeder, nests on ground, well hidden in vegetation.

Quail *Length* 7 in (18 cm). *Call* male, a repeated 'quic, quic-ic', female a wheezing 'queep, queep'. *Habitat* open ground with grass tussocks, rough pasture, crops; resident breeder in south, breeding summer visitor in north.

Pheasant *Length* male 26-35 in (66-89 cm), female 21-24¾ in (53-63 cm). *Call* male with strident 'korrk-kok', both sexes also cackle and chuckle. *Habitat* farm and parkland, woodland edges, reeds; resident breeder, nests on ground: INTRODUCED.

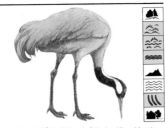

Crane *Length* 44¾ in (114 cm). *Call* a loud 'krooh' and quieter 'kr-r-r' plus various hissing and grating noises. *Habitat* fields, large marshes, steppes, river banks; spring/autumn passage migrant, flying in lines or v-formation.

Little Bustard *Length* 17 in (43 cm). *Call* a short 'dahag' or 'kiak' and a snorting 'ptrr' or 'prett'. *Habitat* grassy plains, large fields of grain, clover; breeding summer visitor, nests on ground.

Water Rail *Length* 11 in (28 cm). *Call* a hard, repeated 'gep-gep-gep', also 'krui, krui, krui', other groaning, squeaking notes. *Habitat* dense aquatic vegetation, reedbeds, weedy ditches; resident breeder, nests in reeds.

Little Crake *Length* 7½ in (19 cm). *Call* a sharp 'quek, quek, quek', gradually deepening, ending in short trill. *Habitat* swamps, fens, pond edges; breeding summer visitor in Massif Central; nests on boggy ground.

Moorhen *Length* 13 in (33 cm). *Call* a harsh 'kr-r-rk' or 'kittick'. *Habitat* ponds, marshes, slow streams, town parks; resident breeder, nests in bushes, reeds near water, often in trees and in old nests of other species.

Coot *Length* 15 in (38 cm). *Call* a distinctive, high 'kowk', 'kewk', and 'cut'; flocks make a communal roaring when alarmed by predator. *Habitat* as for Moorhen but with more open water; resident breeder, nests in reeds, etc.

Oystercatcher *Length* 17 in (43 cm). *Call* a shrill 'kleeep', a shorter 'pic, pic, pic', and a loud, piping communal display call. *Habitat* coastal waters, estuaries, sometimes inland; resident breeder in north, winter visitor in south.

Black-winged Stilt *Length* 15 in (38 cm). *Call* shrill yelping 'kyip, kyip, kyip'. *Habitat* marshes, lagoons, floodwaters; breeding summer visitor in south and Loire region; nests built in shallow water, mud, or on tussock.

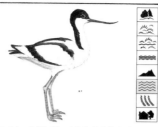

Avocet *Length* 17 in (43 cm). *Call* a high, fluting 'kleep' or 'kloo-it'. *Habitat* mudflats, estuaries, sandbanks; winter visitor on Atlantic and Mediterranean coasts.

Ringed Plover *Length* 6 in (15 cm). *Call* a liquid, musical 'queep' or 'queec', the latter the basis of song in display flight. *Habitat* sandy, muddy shores; resident breeder on Finistère Peninsula, otherwise winter visitor.

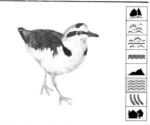

Kentish Plover *Length* 6¼ in (16 cm). *Call* 'wit', 'wee-it', 'prr-ip'. *Habitat* coastal, sandy, and muddy beaches, shingle; resident breeder in north-west, otherwise breeding summer visitor; nests on shingle.

Turnstone *Length* 9 in (23 cm). *Call* a rapid 'tuk-a-tuk' and a long trill. *Habitat* rocky coasts in north and south in winter, otherwise a spring/autumn passage migrant.

Lapwing *Length* 11¾ in (30 cm). *Call* a nasal 'kee-wi', and a longer 'ker-r-wee', with variants in tumbling display flight: 'pee-wi, pee-wit'. *Habitat* farmland, marshes, moors, mudflats; resident breeder, nests on ground.

Redshank *Length* 11 in (28 cm). *Call* a musical slurred 'tleu-hu-hu', yelping cries when alarmed. *Habitat* saltings, marshes, moors; resident tussock nester in Loire and Rhône regions, otherwise a winter coastal visitor and migrant.

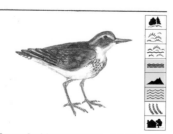

Common Sandpiper *Length* 8 in (20 cm). *Call* high, rapid 'titti-weeti, titti-weeti', a piping 'twee-wee-wee' when alarmed. *Habitat* rivers, hill streams, lakes; resident waterside nester in north-west and south, summer visitor elsewhere.

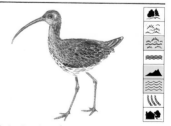

Curlew *Length* 21-22¾ in (53-58 cm). *Call* a pure, ringing 'cour-li', 'crwee', or 'croo-ee'. *Habitat* mudflats, estuaries; resident ground nester in north-west and Massif Central, otherwise a winter visitor.

Woodcock *Length* 13½ in (34 cm). *Call* in slow display flight ('roding') at dawn and dusk, male has soft croaking 'orrrt-orrrt' and high, sneezing 'tsiwick'. *Habitat* woods with wet clearings; resident ground nester.

Stone Curlew *Length* 16 in (41 cm). *Call* mainly in evening, a wailing Curlew-like 'coo-ree' or a shrill 'kee-rrr-eee'. *Habitat* open, dry, stony country, bare, chalky hillsides, heaths; ground-nesting summer visitor.

Collared Pratincole *Length* 10 in (25 cm). *Call* a hard 'kyik' and chattering 'kitti-kirrik-kitik-tik'. *Habitat* marshes, plains, dried mudflats; ground-nesting summer visitor around Rhône delta.

Great Skua *Length* 22¾ in (58 cm). *Call* in flight, 'a-er', when alarmed, a deep 'tuk-tuk'. *Habitat* open seas, coastal waters; a spring/autumn passage migrant along northern coasts, occasional vagrant in Mediterranean.

Arctic Skua *Length* 18 in (46 cm). *Call* a repeated 'ya-wow' in alarm, a nasal, squealing 'ee-air' in flight. *Habitat* open seas, offshore waters; spring/autumn passage migrant along Atlantic and Mediterranean coasts.

Slender-billed Gull *Length* 17 in (43 cm). *Call* a laughing, gull-like 'kau-kau'. *Habitat* coastal waters and estuaries; breeding summer visitor around Rhône Delta, nesting in small groups on mudbanks, lagoon islands, marshes.

Black-headed Gull *Length* 13¾-15 in (35-38 cm). *Call* a harsh, raucous 'kraah'. *Habitat* coastal regions and inland, frequenting lakes, harbours, farms; resident breeder in eastern half of country, otherwise a winter visitor.

Little Gull *Length* 11 in (28 cm). *Call* a repeated 'ka-ka-ka', with a harsh 'kek-kek-kek'. *Habitat* as for Black-headed Gull; a winter visitor in coastal regions, otherwise a spring/autumn passage migrant.

Mediterranean Gull *Length* 15½ in (39 cm). *Call* a deep 'kek-ke-ke', 'kee-er' or 'kau-kau-kyau'. *Habitat* as for Black-headed Gull, though less often seen inland; a winter visitor to Atlantic and Mediterranean coasts.

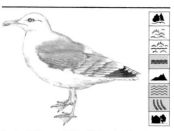

Herring Gull *Length* 22-26 in (56-66 cm). *Call* a yelping 'kee-yow' and in spring also, a loud 'gah-gah-gah'. *Habitat* coastal waters, estuaries, fields, often far inland; resident breeder, colonial nesting on cliffs, islands, beaches.

Lesser Black-backed Gull *Length* 21-22 in (53-56 cm). *Call* like a deep, gruff Herring Gull. *Habitat* as for Herring Gull; resident breeder on Finistère Peninsula, nests colonially on cliff tops, moors, bogs, winter visitor elsewhere.

Greater Black-backed Gull *Length* 25¼-31 in (64-79 cm). *Call* a deep, harsh 'owk'. *Habitat* resident breeder on Finistère Peninsula, nesting colonially on rocky coastal islands, moors, cliffs, elsewhere, a winter coastal visitor.

Common Gull *Length* 16 in (41 cm). *Call* a weaker, high-pitched version of the Herring Gull's 'kee-yow'. *Habitat* coastal waters, estuaries, very often inland; winter visitor except for central areas.

Kittiwake *Length* 16 in (41 cm). *Call* loud cries of 'kitt-ee-wayke' and a low 'uk-uk' and a wailing note. *Habitat* open seas, often at fishing grounds, often follows ships; winters around coast, summer breeder on Finistère, nests on steep cliffs.

Gull-billed Tern *Length* 15 in (38 cm). *Call* a distinct 'quac-quac-quac' and 'cher-wuc'. *Habitat* sandy coasts, salt marshes, inland waters; breeding resident in south, nests colonially on lagoon islets and sandy shores.

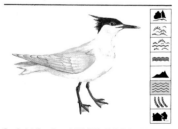

Sandwich Tern *Length* 16 in (41 cm). *Call* a loud, harsh 'kirrick' or 'kirr-whit'. *Habitat* almost entirely marine; summer breeder on Cherbourg and Finistère Peninsulas, colonial nesting on sand, shingle beaches, elsewhere a passage migrant.

Common Tern *Length* 13¾ in (35 cm). *Call* high-pitched, strident, usually 'keeerree', 'keeyah', and 'kik-kik-kik'. *Habitat* coastal and inland waters; summer breeder, nests colonially on dunes, beaches, and islands.

Little Tern *Length* 9½ in (24 cm). *Call* mainly a high, rasping 'kik-kik' and 'pee-e-eer', plus trills. *Habitat* coastal waters, sand, shingle beaches; breeding summer visitor, nests on beaches, shores of rivers, and lakes.

Razorbill *Length* 16 in (41 cm). *Call* only at breeding grounds, a weak, whirring whistle and a growling 'arrr'. *Habitat* offshore and coastal waters in winter, a breeding summer visitor on cliffs on Cherbourg and Finistère Peninsulas.

Guillemot *Length* 16½ in (42 cm). *Call* in breeding season, a loud, harsh 'arrr' or 'arra'. *Habitat* offshore and coastal waters; breeding summer visitor on Cherbourg and Finistère Peninsulas, nests on steep cliffs, elsewhere a winter visitor.

Puffin *Length* 11¾ in (30 cm). *Call* usually silent, but a low growling note at nest sites. *Habitat* coastal and offshore waters, where a spring/autumn passage migrant; breeding summer visitor in north-west, nests in holes.

Rock Dove or Feral Pigeon *Length* 13 in (33 cm). *Call* 'oo-roo-coo'. *Habitat* rocky sea cliffs, nearby fields; domestic forms common in cities; resident breeder in north-west and along Mediterranean coast, nests in rock crevices.

Stock Dove *Length* 13 in (33 cm). *Call* 'ooo-roo-oo', like Wood Pigeon, but more monotonous. *Habitat* cliffs, sand-dunes, preferring open parkland; resident breeder, nests in tree holes, rocks, rabbit burrows.

Wood Pigeon or Ring Dove *Length* 16 in (41 cm). *Call* 'coo-coo-roo, coo-coo', muffled and repeated. *Habitat* almost anywhere with trees; resident breeder, nesting in hedges, trees, and old nests.

Collared Dove *Length* 12½ in (32 cm). *Call* a deep 'coo-cooo, coo', in flight, a nasal 'hwee'. *Habitat* town and village gardens, a recent colonist from 1950s; resident breeder in eastern half of country, nests in trees.

Turtle Dove *Length* 10½ in (27 cm). *Call* soft, a repeated, purring 'roor-r-r'. *Habitat* various, open woodland, scattered trees; breeding summer visitor, nesting in scrubby thickets, bushes, orchards.

Great Spotted Cuckoo *Length* 15½ in (39 cm). *Call* a harsh grating 'keeow-keeow-keeow-keeow' and a crow-like alarm call. *Habitat* scrubby plains, woodland glades and edges; summer visitor, eggs reared in crows' nests.

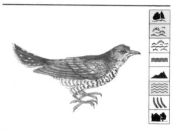

Cuckoo *Length* 13 in (33 cm). *Call* male, the familiar 'cuc-coo' and a deep 'wow-wow-wow'; female a long bubbly note. *Habitat* various, moors, dunes, forests; breeding summer visitor, young reared by various bird species.

Barn Owl *Length* 13½ in (34 cm). *Call* long, wild shriek, also, hisses, barks, snores. *Habitat* open, often dry country, with scattered trees; a resident breeder, often nesting in old barns, outhouses, and churches; food mainly rodents.

Eagle Owl *Length* 26-28 in (66-71 cm). *Call* short deep 'ooo-hu', a sharp 'kveck, kveck'. *Habitat* crags, steppes, rocky outcrops in forests; resident breeder in south, nests in rock crevices, hollow trees, old bird-of-prey nests.

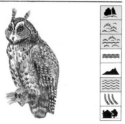

Long-eared Owl *Length* 14 in (36 cm). *Call* a long, sighing 'oo-oo-oo', also, yelping and wailing notes and wing clapping. *Habitat* coniferous forests, marshes, heaths, dunes, areas with scattered trees; resident breeder in old nests.

Scops Owl *Length* 7½ in (19 cm). *Call* a melancholy whistling 'kyew'. *Habitat* open woodland, farmland, open country with scattered trees; breeding summer visitor, nests in old birds' nests or holes.

Little Owl *Length* 8¾ in (22 cm). *Call* a barking 'werro' and a shrill 'kiu'. *Habitat* open country with scattered trees, farmland, orchards, dunes; breeding resident, nests in tree holes, burrows, among rocks.

Tawny Owl *Length* 15 in (38 cm). *Call* a shrill 'ke-wick', also, a deep 'hoo-hoo-hoo' followed by a wavering 'oo-oo-oo-oo'. *Habitat* open woodland, areas with scattered trees, large gardens; resident, nests in holes, old nests.

Swift *Length* 6½ in (16.5 cm). *Call* a prolonged shrill screech, chirping at nest. *Habitat* aerial, in areas suitable for nesting; breeding summer visitor, nesting under eaves of buildings, on rocky cliffs, sometimes in tree holes.

Pallid Swift *Length* 6½ in (16.5 cm). *Call* as for Swift. *Habitat* as for Swift, with which it often associates; breeding summer visitor, distinguished from Swift by distinctly paler-brown and larger, white throat patch.

Alpine Swift *Length* 8¾ in (22 cm). *Call* in flight, a chorus of loud, rising and falling trilling whistles. *Habitat* high mountainous areas, seacliffs; breeding summer visitor, cup-shaped nest in crevices, rock clefts, in colonies.

Bee-eater *Length* 11 in (28 cm). *Call* in flight, a rather liquid 'quilp', also a throaty 'kroop, kroop'. *Habitat* open bushy country, sometimes woodland glades; breeding summer visitor in south, nests in holes in banks, sandy cliffs.

Roller *Length* 12¼ in (31 cm). *Call* a loud, deep, crow-like 'kr-r-r-r-ak' or 'krak-ak'. *Habitat* open country with scattered trees, mature forests; breeding summer visitor in south, nests in hollow trees, ruins, holes in banks.

Kingfisher *Length* 6½ in (16.5 cm). *Call* a loud, shrill 'cheee' or 'chikeee'. *Habitat* fresh waters of all kinds in lowland areas, estuaries and coasts in winter; resident breeder, nests excavated in stream and river banks.

Hoopoe *Length* 11 in (28 cm). *Call* rapid, clipped, 'hoo-hoo-hoo', also several mewing notes and, in alarm, a quiet chattering. *Habitat* open woodlands, grassy plains, farms, orchards; breeding summer visitor, nests in holes in trees.

Black Woodpecker *Length* 18 in (46 cm). *Call* in flight, a loud ringing 'choc-choc-choc'. Also a high 'krri-krri-krri'. *Habitat* mature conifer forests in mountain areas, and beechwoods; resident breeder, large nest hole high in trees.

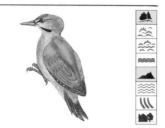

Grey-headed Woodpecker *Length* 10 in (25 cm). *Call* similar to 'laughing' of Green Woodpecker, but deeper, less harsh. *Habitat* deciduous woods, including mountainous areas, in eastern half; nests in tree holes.

Green Woodpecker *Length* 12½ in (32 cm). *Call* a loud, ringing 'laugh': 'plue-plue-plue', sometimes loud, yelping cries. *Habitat* broadleaved and mixed forests, parks, gardens; will feed on ground, lawns, anthills; nests in tree holes.

Great Spotted or Pied Woodpecker *Length* 9 in (23 cm). *Call* a loud, sharp, 'tchick' or 'kik'; both sexes drum rapidly on dead branches. *Habitat* woodlands, including pinewoods; resident breeder, nests in tree holes.

Middle Spotted Woodpecker *Length* 8¾ in (22 cm). *Call* a repeated 'kik' note and a slow rising or falling 'wait, wait'. *Habitat* usually in high branches of broadleaved and coniferous woodland; resident, nests in high tree hole.

Crested Lark *Length* 6¾ in (17 cm). *Call* a rising and falling, liquid 'twee-tee-too', in short, repeated bursts in flight, from perch or on ground. *Habitat* dry, stony, sandy wastes, roadsides; resident ground nester.

Swallow *Length* 7½ in (19 cm). *Call* a high 'tswit', which becomes a rapid twitter in excitement; a high 'tswee' when alarmed. *Habitat* open farmland with ponds; breeding summer visitor, open mud and straw nests on rafters, ledges.

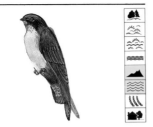

Crag Martin *Length* 5¾ in (14.5 cm). *Call* rarely vocal; a weak 'chich' or 'tchrri'. *Habitat* rocky inland and coastal cliffs, mountain gorges, though rarely at high altitudes; resident breeder in south, open mud nests in rock clefts.

Sand Martin *Length* 4¾ in (12 cm). *Call* a reedy 'tchrrip', in alarm, a short 'brrit', less musical than Swallow. *Habitat* open country with ponds, rivers; breeding summer visitor, nests communally in tunnels in sand, gravel banks.

Tawny Pipit *Length* 6½ in (16.5 cm). *Call* variants of 'tzeep', 'tzi-uc', louder than other pipits. *Habitat* dry, open, sandy areas, heaths, dunes, hillsides; breeding summer visitor, nest on ground in scrape sheltered by vegetation.

White Wagtail *Length* 7 in (18 cm). *Call* a high-pitched 'tschizzick', in alarm, 'tchik'; otherwise variants of call. *Habitat* open country, often in farmland and near freshwater; resident, nests in rock crevices, buildings.

Lesser Grey Shrike *Length* 8 in (20 cm). *Call* harsh 'shek-shek' with also a clear 'kviell'. *Habitat* open country with scattered trees and bushes, roadsides; breeding summer visitor, nests in high trees, near to trunk.

Woodchat Shrike *Length* 6¾ in (17 cm). *Call* harsh and variable 'shek-shek' with sparrow-like chatter, otherwise, a musical, warbling song mixed with harsh notes. *Habitat* dry open country; summer visitor, nests in trees.

Alpine Accentor *Length* 7 in (18 cm). *Call* 'tchir-rip' and a throaty 'churrg', with a sustained warbling song. *Habitat* rocky mountain slopes and crags, wintering in lowlands; resident, nests in vegetation or rock holes.

Grasshopper Warbler *Length* 5 in (13 cm). *Call* a short 'twhit' or 'pitt', with distinctive, far-carrying, grasshopper-like churring. *Habitat* undergrowth; ground-nesting summer visitor.

Savi's Warbler *Length* 5½ in (14 cm). *Call* a quiet 'tswik' and scolding chatter, with song of low, reeling trills. *Habitat* marshy areas, reedbeds with bushes; breeding summer visitor, nest well hidden in tangled dead reeds, sedges.

Marsh Warbler *Length* 5 in (12.5 cm). *Call* a loud 'tchuc', a quiet 'tuc', with a very musical, canary-like song. *Habitat* dense vegetation near water; summer visitor, nests in low herbage.

Cetti's Warbler *Length* 5½ in (14 cm). *Call* 'chee', 'twic', 'huit', and churring note; loud staccato song of 'chewee, chewee, cheweeweeweewee' or 'pit, pit, pitpit'. *Habitat* dense waterside vegetation, where nests are well hidden.

Blackcap *Length* 5½ in (14 cm). *Call* a sharp 'tac, tac', rapidly repeated in alarm and a harsh churring; song a rich warble. *Habitat* woodland glades with undergrowth, hedges, orchards; resident breeder, nests in brambles, evergreens.

Sardinian Warbler *Length* 5¼ in (13.5 cm). *Call* in alarm, a loud, sharp 'cha-cha-cha-cha'; song a mixture of musical notes and snatches of alarm call. *Habitat* dry, open, scrubby areas; resident breeder in south, nests in undergrowth.

Goldcrest *Length* 3½ in (9 cm). *Call* a high, frequent 'zee-zee-zee'; song a thin, high, double note ending in short twitter. *Habitat* coniferous and mixed woodland, undergrowth; breeding resident, nest suspended under tip of branch.

Spotted Flycatcher *Length* 5½ in (14 cm). *Call* a shrill 'tzee', a rapid 'tzee, tuc-tuc'; song a few thin notes. *Habitat* woodland edges, parks, gardens; breeding summer visitor, nest against tree trunk, on building.

Blue Rock Thrush *Length* 8 in (20 cm). *Call* a hard 'tchuck' or a plaintive 'tsec'; loud fluty song especially in morning and at sunset. *Habitat* resident in south, nests in rock crevices, cliffs, buildings.

Rock Thrush *Length* 7½ in (19 cm). *Call* 'chack, chack' and a clear, piping song. *Habitat* open rocky areas from 1-2600 m, sometimes lower among trees and ruins; breeding summer visitor in south.

Black-eared Wheatear *Length* 5¾ in (14.5 cm). *Call* a rasping note; otherwise, song a lark-like warbling preceded by a soft 'plit'. *Habitat* stony slopes, dry, open, lightly wooded country; breeding summer visitor, nests in rock crevices.

Black Wheatear *Length* 7 in (18 cm). *Call* short, sweet warbling, starting and ending with a chatter. *Habitat* dry, rocky places, cliffs, gorges; resident in south, nests in holes in rocks, often screened by wall of pebbles.

Bearded Tit *Length* 6½ in (16.5 cm). *Call* a metallic 'ching', 'dzu-dzu', and a kissing note. *Habitat* confined to very large reedbeds; resident breeder in Rhône Delta, low nest near edge of reedbed.

Rock Bunting *Length* 6¼ in (16 cm). *Call* a sharp 'tzit'; song a high-pitched, buzzing 'zi-zi-zi-zirr'. *Habitat* rocky mountains and hillsides, wintering on low ground; resident breeder, nests on or near ground.

Chaffinch *Length* 6 in (15 cm). *Call* in flight, a soft 'tsip', otherwise, a repeated, loud 'pink, pink'; song a very variable cascade of notes. *Habitat* woods, gardens, farmland; resident, nests low in tree or bush.

Golden Oriole *Length* 9½ in (24 cm). *Call* male, a loud, fluting 'weela-weeo', both sexes also a cat-like squawk, in alarm, a harsh 'chr-r-r'. *Habitat* broadleaved woods and forests, large gardens; summer visitor, nests high in trees.

Alpine Chough *Length* 15 in (38 cm). *Call* similar to Chough's, but notes more monosyllabic, a distinct, metallic 'chirrish'. *Habitat* high mountains with steep cliffs; resident in south and south-west, nests in rock clefts.

Common Frog *Length* 3-4 in (8-10 cm). *Call* a quiet 'grook-grook-grook' during mating season. *Habitat* ponds, when breeding, often in gardens; at other times in damp vegetation in marshy areas, along river and stream banks.

Edible Frog *Length* 4-4¾ in (10-12 cm). *Call* variable, includes mixture of several songs like the rasping 'croax-croax' and the more rapid 'bre-ke-ke-ke-kek'. *Habitat* ponds and lakes, and in damp places.

Common Toad *Length* 5-6 in (13-15 cm). *Call* a short harsh 'qwark-qwark-qwark' heard around dusk and at night. *Habitat* under stones and logs in fields, woodland, and gardens; emerge at night. In ponds, in large numbers, in breeding season.

Natterjack Toad *Length* 2½-4 in (6-10 cm). *Call* short, loud, repetitive croak; several males form a chorus. *Habitat* in sandy areas; burrows in loose sand during day and emerges to feed at night. Breeds in brackish pools.

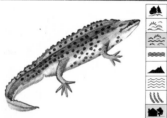

Smooth or Common Newt *Length* 2½-4 in (6-10 cm) with tail; females smaller than males. *Colour* variable; breeding males develop dorsal crest and bright-orange belly. *Habitat* shallow ponds and ditches in spring; rest of year in damp places.

Palmate Newt *Length* 2¾-3½ in (7-9 cm) with tail; males smaller than females. *Colour* variable; breeding males develop tail crest and yellow belly. *Habitat* shallow, open ponds and lakes in spring; at other times in vegetation near water.

Slow Worm *Length* 17¾-20 in (45-50 cm). *Colour* variable; juveniles brighter with golden scales; males with scattered blue spots. A legless lizard. *Habitat* under logs and stones in damp grassland, woods, and embankments.

Viviparous or Common Lizard *Length* 4¾-7 in (12-18 cm) including tail. *Colour* variable brown to green with dark spots or stripes; breeding male with orange or red belly. *Habitat* damp meadows, woods in south, but drier heaths, sand-dunes in north.

Sand Lizard *Length* 6¼-10 in (16-25 cm). *Colour* very variable; juvenile brown with white spots, male with bright-green sides, some forms with red dorsal stripe. *Habitat* dry sandy areas with plant cover; dry embankments in south.

Common Wall Lizard *Length* 7-8¾ in (18-22 cm) including tail. *Colour* very variable; males conspicuous spotted pattern with orange belly; southern forms black with green spots. *Habitat* dry, sunny walls, rockfaces; often in or near houses.

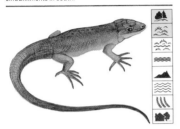

Green Lizard *Length* 11¾-15¾ in (30-40 cm) with tail. *Colour* variable in females from green to brown; juvenile males without blue chin. *Habitat* wooded or scrubby areas in south; heathland in north.

Adder *Length* 23½-31½ in (60-80 cm). *Bite* CAN BE FATAL. *Colour* very variable, and typical zig-zag pattern may be absent; males more strongly marked. *Habitat* moist heaths, moorland and open woods. Active in day.

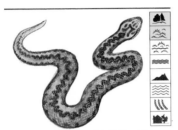

Smooth Snake *Length* 23½-27½ in (60-70 cm). *Colour* variable from grey to red; distinguish from vipers by smoother, less-prominent head scales. *Habitat* dry, open, stony areas in south, woodland or scrub in north.

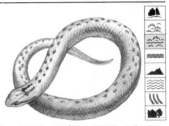

Grass Snake *Length* 39½-71 in (100-180 cm). *Colour* variable from green to brown or grey; pale or yellow collar. *Habitat* mainly damp places near water; swims quite readily. May feign death if disturbed.

Aesculapian Snake *Length* 53-78¾ in (135-200 cm). *Colour* variable; juveniles with dark spots. *Habitat* mainly sunny, sheltered places in woodland and shrubby areas; good climbers, so found in trees and old walls.

Asp Viper *Length* 23½-29½ (60-75 cm). *Bite* CAN BE FATAL. *Colour* some forms completely black, especially in north. *Habitat* mainly dry stony areas, cultivated fields and vineyards; occasionally in cooler mountain regions.

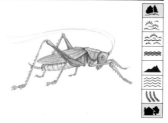

Oak Bush Cricket *Length* ½-⅗ in (3.5-15.5 mm). *Song* males only, soft chirping by rubbing wing bases together, *or* drumming with one of hind legs. *Habitat* oakwoods in summer, where it preys on other insects; often attracted to light at night.

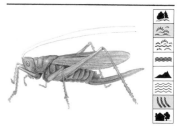

Great Green Bush Cricket *Length* 1½-2 in (40-50 mm). *Song* males only, a prolonged, harsh chirping, like sound of bicycle freewheeling. *Habitat* shrubby areas with long grasses, feeding on small insects and plant material, in summer.

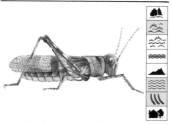

German Grasshopper *Length* ⅔-1 1/10 (17-28 mm). *Song* males only, a regular, rasping chirp. *Habitat* dry hillsides, *garrigue* vegetation, feeding on low plants and plant debris; readily takes to flight, exposing red hindwings, in summer.

Common Field Grasshopper *Length* ⅗-9/10 in (15-23 mm). *Song* short, brisk chirp, males only. *Habitat* open, dry, stony areas, dry agricultural land, woodland clearings, sand-dunes, in summer.

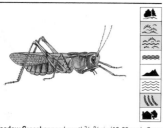

Meadow Grasshopper *Length* ⅖-9/10 in (10-22 mm). *Song* regular bursts of quiet chirping, males only. *Habitat* a wide range, including nearly all forms of grassland which are not too heavily grazed, heathland, marshy areas, in summer.

Mottled Grasshopper *Length* ½-⅘ in (12-19 mm). *Song* males only, 10-30 rapidly repeated chirps, louder towards end. *Habitat* dry heaths, sandy areas, including dunes, dry pasture and waste ground, flies readily, in summer.

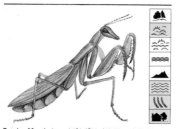

Praying Mantis *Length* 1½-2¾ in (40-70 mm). *Habitat* bushes and low vegetation almost everywhere in the south, sitting still for long periods in attitude of 'prayer', waiting to grasp insect prey with powerful, raptorial front legs.

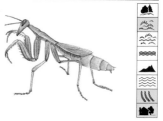

Lesser Praying Mantis *Length* 1⅖-1½ in (36-40 mm). *Habitat* small bushes and trees in dry, stony areas from August onwards; not so common as Praying Mantis.

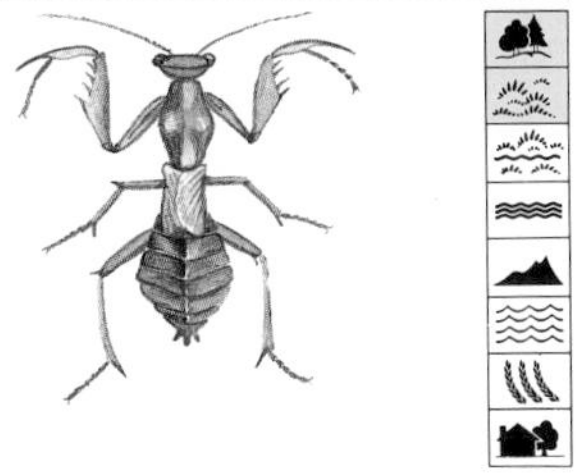

Small Mantis *Length* 4/5-1 in (20-25 mm). *Habitat* in groves of Evergreen Oak, in autumn, sometimes on dry ground, where well camouflaged, in the south.

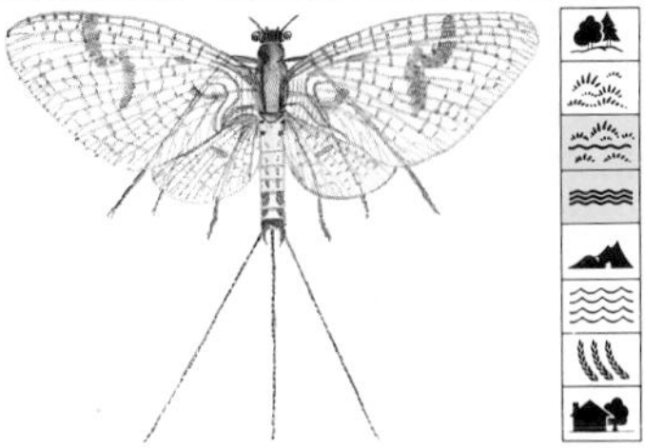

Common Mayfly *Wingspan* 1 3/4 in (45 mm). *Habitat* waterside vegetation, especially near slow-flowing rivers and canals; dense mating swarms immediately after emergence in May; known to fly fishers as the 'drake'.

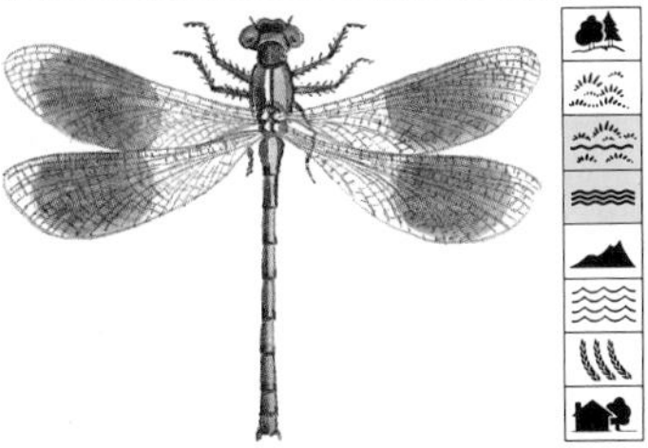

Splendid Damselfly *Length* male abdomen 1 1/4-1 1/2 in (33-39 mm), hindwing 1 1/10-1 1/4 in (27-32 mm); female abdomen 1 1/4-1 3/5 in (33-40 mm), hindwing 1 1/5-1 2/5 in (31-36 mm). *Habitat* slow-flowing rivers, ponds, still waters. *Season* May-end September.

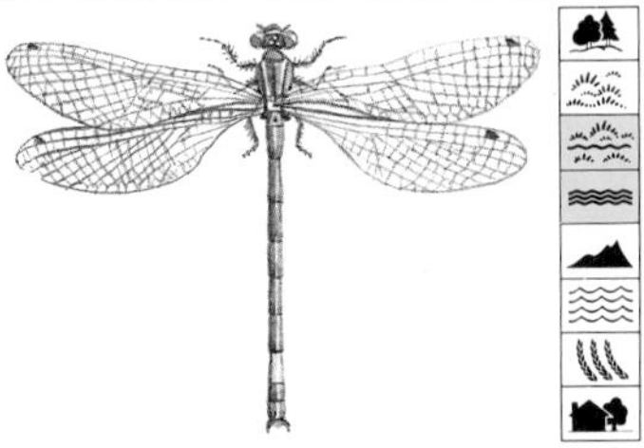

Elegant Damselfly *Length* male abdomen 9/10-1 1/10 in (22-28 mm), hindwing 3/5-1 1/10 in (14-18 mm); female abdomen 9/10-1 1/10 in (22-29 mm), hindwing 3/5-4/5 in (15-20 mm). *Habitat* near stagnant or slow-flowing waters, below 3300 ft (1000 m). *Season* end March-end October.

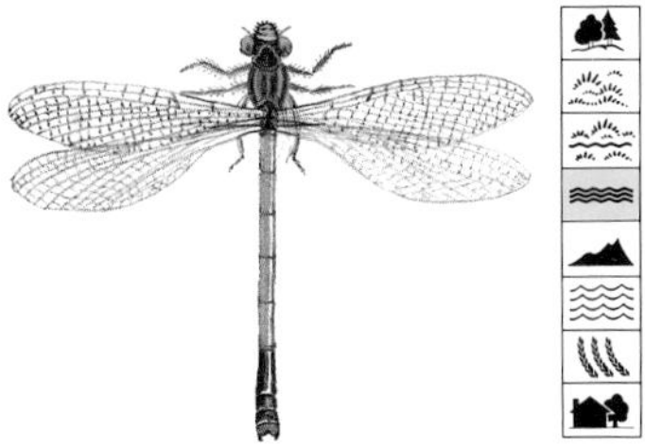

Red Damselfly *Length* male abdomen 1-1 1/10 in (25-29 mm), hindwing 4/5-9/10 in (19-22 mm); female abdomen 1-1 1/10 in (26-28 mm), hindwing 4/5-1 1/10 in (21-24 mm). *Habitat* around small, clear streams, ponds, lakes, etc, up to 4000 ft (1200 m). *Season* April-September.

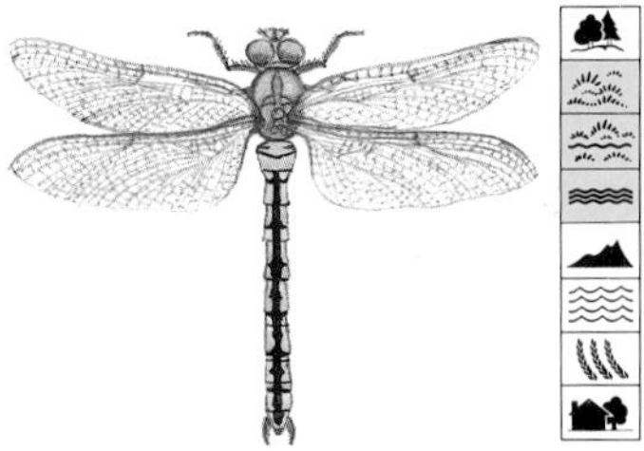

Emperor Dragonfly *Length* male abdomen 2 1/10-2 2/5 in (53-61 mm), hindwing 1 3/4-2 in (45-50 mm); female abdomen 1 9/10-2 1/4 in (49-57 mm), hindwing 1 4/5-2 in (46-51 mm). *Habitat* around ponds, lakes, stagnant ditches, but very often far from water. *Season* May-September.

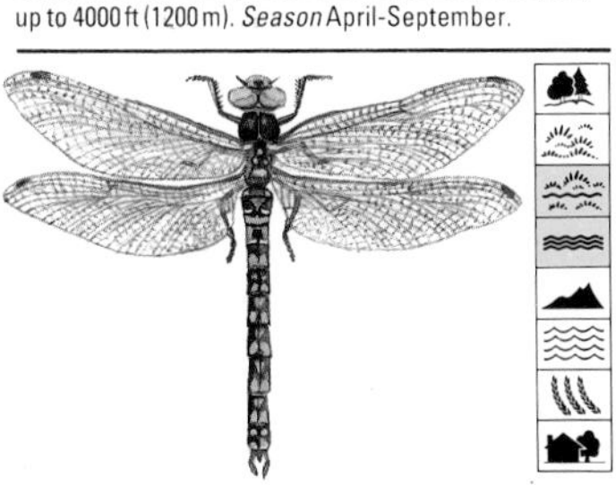

Migrant Hawker Dragonfly *Length* male abdomen 1 3/4-1 9/10 in (44-49 mm), hindwing 1 1/2 in (37-39 mm); female abdomen 1 2/3-1 9/10 in (43-48 mm), hindwing 1 1/2-1 3/5 in (38-40 mm). *Habitat* around slow-flowing waters, often far from water. *Season* June-October.

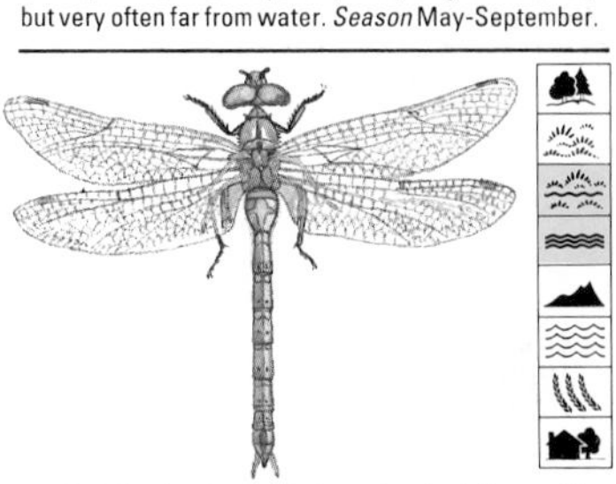

Norfolk Hawker Dragonfly *Length* male abdomen 1 4/5-2 in (47-50 mm), hindwing 1 1/2-1 2/3 in (39-42 mm); female abdomen 2-2 1/10 in (50-54 mm), hindwing 1 3/5-1 3/4 in (41-45 mm). *Habitat* usually around stagnant waters, not often far from water. *Season* May-August.

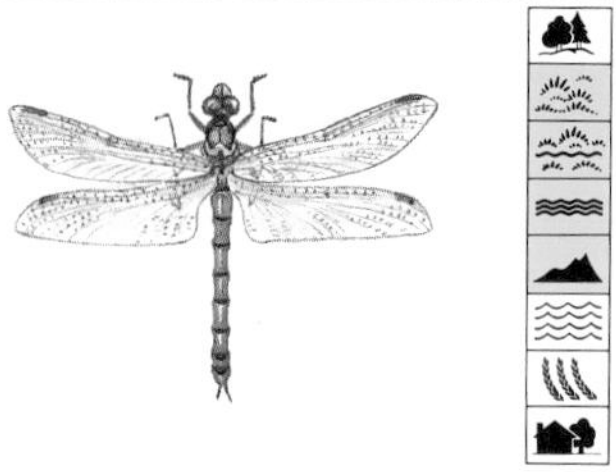

Common Darter Dragonfly. *Length* male abdomen 1-1½in (25-30mm), hindwing 1-1½in (25-30mm); female abdomen 1-1½in (25-29mm), hindwing 1-1½in (26-30mm). *Habitat* around stagnant water, peat bogs, streams to 6000ft (1800m). *Season* May-October.

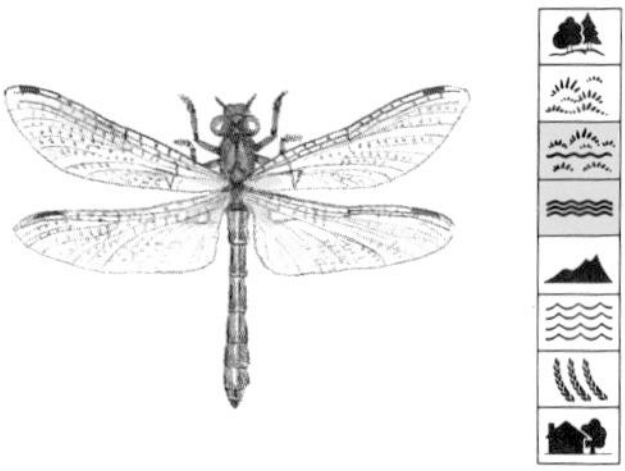

Ruddy Darter Dragonfly *Length* male abdomen ⅘-9/10in (20-24mm), hindwing 9/10-1 1/10in (23-28mm); female abdomen 9/10-1in (22-26mm), hindwing 1-1 1/10in (25-29mm). *Habitat* near stagnant, acid waters, ponds, peat bogs. *Season* June-early October.

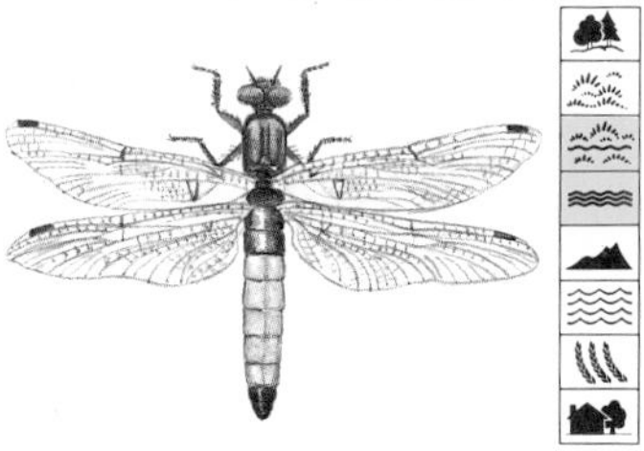

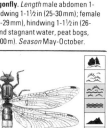

Black-tailed Skimmer Dragonfly *Length* male abdomen 1⅕-1⅓ (30-35mm), hindwing 1⅓-1⅗in (35-40mm); female abdomen 1 1/10-1⅓in (29-34mm), hindwing 1⅓-1⅗in (35-41mm). *Habitat* near ponds, lakes, peat bogs. *Season* April-end of September.

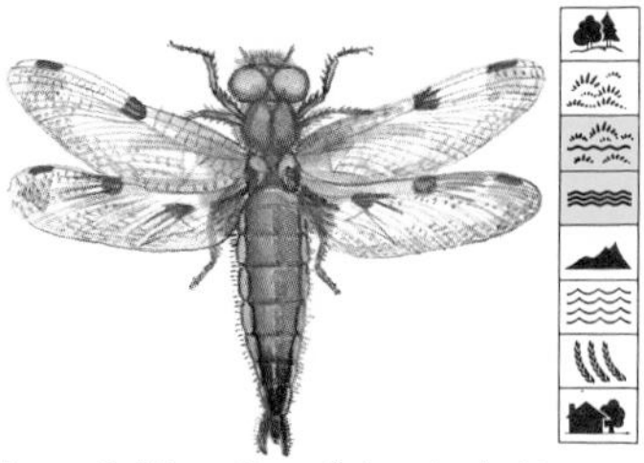

Four-spotted Chaser Dragonfly *Length* male abdomen 1 1/10-1¼in (27-32mm), hindwing 1¼-1⅖in (32-36mm); female abdomen 1 1/10-1⅕in (28-31mm), hindwing 1½-1½in (33-39mm). *Habitat* near weedy, stagnant waters, up to 6575ft (2000mm). *Season* April-September.

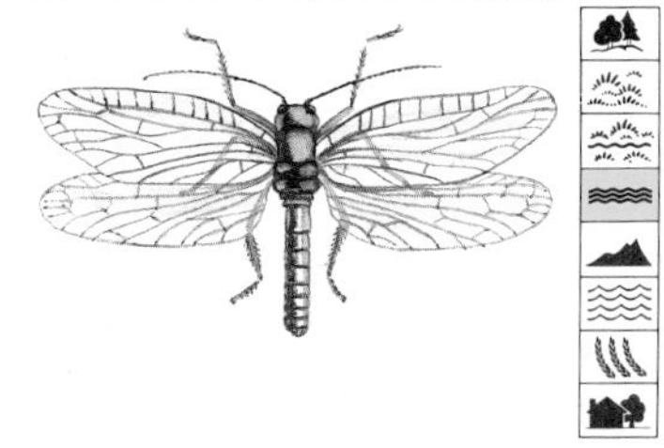

Common Alderfly *Length* including folded wings, about ⅗in (15mm). *Habitat* vegetation around the margins of lakes, slow streams; eggs laid in masses on plants over water, larvae drop on hatching and live on muddy bottom.

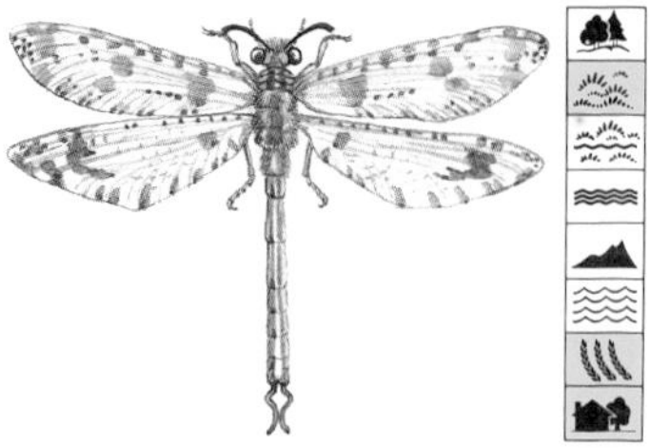

Ant Lion *Length* abdomen 1½in (37mm), wingspan 1⅘in (47mm). *Habitat* dry, stony hillsides, adult with characteristic 'lazy' rising and falling flight; name from larvae which excavate pits in sand and feed on insects, mainly ants, which fall in.

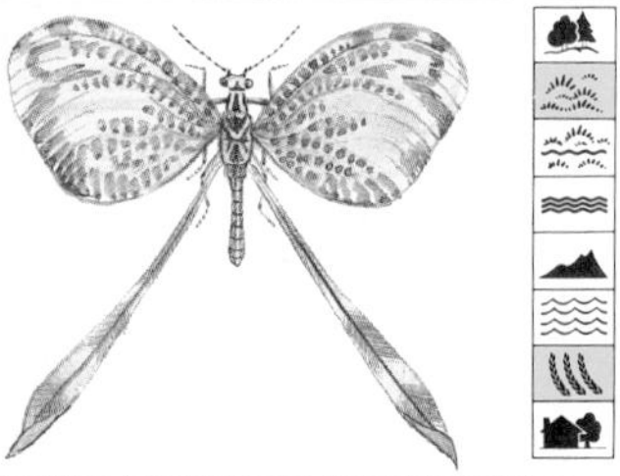

Ribbon Wing *Length* including ribbon-like hindwings 1⅔-1⅘in (43-45mm). *Habitat* warm, dry, open country, flying at dusk with characteristic, bobbing action; larvae in caves, outbuildings, feeding on other insects.

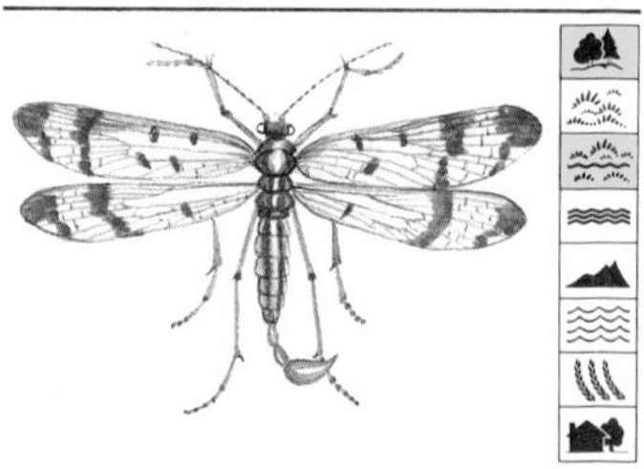

Common Scorpionfly *Length* including wings at rest, ⅗-⅘in (16-20mm). *Habitat* lush vegetation in damp, shady places, often seen walking over leaves, where they feed on dead or dying insects, insect remains in spider webs, in summer.

Harlequin Spittlebug *Length* 1/3-1/2 in (9-12mm). *Habitat* rank, lush vegetation along roadsides, woodland clearings and edges, hedgerows, margins of cultivated land; common throughout the summer.

Harlequin Shieldbug *Length* 1/3-2/5 in (9-11mm). *Habitat* found mainly on umbellifers, sucking sap, among roadside vegetation, marginal areas and waste grounds; common in summer months.

Spiny Squashbug *Length* 1/3-2/5 in (9-10mm). *Habitat* dry, stony, open country, usually found on papery flowers of Silvery Paronychia or dry flowerheads of Lavender, against which it is well camouflaged; common in summer.

Ground Bug *Length* 2/5 in (10-11mm). *Habitat* open country, roadside vegetation, on a variety of plants and also around the margins of cultivated land; common throughout summer.

 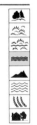

Assassin Bug *Length* 2/5 in (10-11mm). *Habitat* vegetation including flowers, in marginal areas of woods, fields, cultivated plots, where it preys on other insects; often walks about with prey impaled on sucking mouthparts, in summer.

Common Backswimmer *Length* 2/5-1/2 in (10-12mm). *Habitat* weedy, slow-moving rivers, canals, also ponds, where it feeds on aquatic vegetation; flies readily in hot weather and often is attracted to light at night; from January onwards.

Common Water Boatman *Length* 1/2-3/5 in (13-15mm). *Habitat* ponds, ditches, drainage canals, voracious predator of small animals, killing them with an injection of toxic saliva from the piercing and sucking mouthparts; all year.

Firebug *Length* 1/3-2/5 in (8-10.5mm). *Habitat* on Mallows and Lime trees, feeding on seeds though sometimes carnivorous and will prey on small insects; also, mating pairs often seen running on bare ground; April-May.

Swallowtail *Description* male forewing 1¼-1½ in (32-38 mm); sexes similar. *Flight* 2 broods, April/May, July/August. *Habitat* flowery meadows and banks, sea-level to 6600 ft (2000 m). *Larvae* on Wild Carrot, Fennel, and other umbellifers.

Corsican Swallowtail *Description* male forewing 1⅖-1½ in (36-38 mm); sexes similar, very like Swallowtail, but tails shorter. *Flight* May-July. *Habitat* mountains 2000-4275 ft (600-1300 m), Corsica and Sardinia only. *Larvae* on umbellifers.

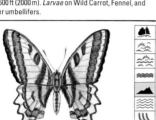

Southern Swallowtail *Description* male forewing 1⅕-1¼ in (31-33 mm); female often larger, otherwise similar. *Flight* April-July. *Habitat* mountainous areas up to 4300 ft (1300 m), attracted to thistles in south. *Larvae* on umbellifers.

Scarce Swallowtail *Description* male forewing 1¼-1⅗ in (32-40 mm), female larger; wing patterns vary. *Flight* March-September. *Habitat* lowlands to 6600 ft (2000 m) or higher, flying around orchards. *Larvae* on sloe, cultivated fruit.

Southern Festoon *Description* male forewing ⁹⁄₁₀-1 in (23-26 mm); sexes similar. *Flight* single brooded, end April/May. *Habitat* rough, stony areas, from lowlands to 3300 ft (1000 m). *Larvae* on Birthwort plants.

Apollo *Description* 1⅓-1⅔ in (35-42 mm); sexes similar except females may have red spots larger. *Flight* July-August. *Habitat* mountain regions at subalpine levels, from 2750-6600 ft (830-2000 m). *Larvae* on Stonecrop.

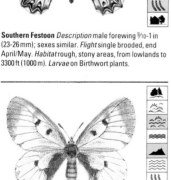

Clouded Apollo *Description* male forewing 1-1⅕ in (26-31 mm); sexes similar, though some females with dark suffusions on wings. *Flight* single brooded, May-July. *Habitat* damp meadows in hills and mountains up to 5500 ft (1650 m). *Larvae* on corydalis.

Large White (Cabbage White) *Description* male forewing 1¹⁄₁₀-1¼ in (28-33 mm); female hindwing yellow tinged. *Flight* April/May, and July/August. *Habitat* gardens, flowery waysides, and fields up to 6600 ft (2000 m). *Larvae* on Cabbage and related plants.

Peak White *Description* male forewing ⅘-1 in (21-26 mm); female with stronger dark markings. *Flight* late June-August. *Habitat* alpine, grassy slopes from 6900 ft (2100 m) upwards. *Larvae* on Smooth Mignonette and alpine cabbage family.

Brimstone *Description* male forewing 1-1⅕ in (26-30 mm); female wing markings similar, wings greenish white. *Flight* June, hibernated individuals appearing following spring. *Habitat* open areas to 6600 ft (2000 m). *Larvae* on Buckthorn.

Nettle-tree Butterfly *Description* male forewing ⅔-⁹⁄₁₀ in (17-22 mm); females similar; colour pattern very constant. *Flight* June-August/September, March/April. *Habitat* lowlands up to 1650 ft (500 m), usually near Nettle-trees. *Larvae* on Nettle-tree.

Two-tailed Pasha *Description* male forewing 1½-1⅗ in (38-41 mm); female similar, larger. *Flight* two broods, May/June and August/September. *Habitat* from sea-level to 1650 ft (500 m). *Larvae* on Strawberry Tree.

Southern White Admiral *Description* male forewing ⁹⁄₁₀-1¹⁄₁₀ in (23-27 mm); female similar. *Flight* two or three broods, beginning in May. *Habitat* scrub, open woodlands from sea-level to treeline. *Larvae* on Honeysuckle.

Camberwell Beauty *Description* male forewing 1⅕-1⅓ in (30-34 mm); female similar. *Flight* June/July and again in spring after hibernation. *Habitat* open, usually hilly or mountainous country. *Larvae* willows, birch, other deciduous forest trees.

Peacock *Description* male forewing 1¹⁄₁₀ in (27-29 mm); female similar, slightly larger. *Flight* July onwards, again in spring after hibernation. *Habitat* flowery areas to 6600 ft (2000 m). *Larvae* usually on nettles.

Red Admiral *Description* male forewing 1¹⁄₁₀-1⅕ in (28-31 mm); female similar. *Flight* May-October, in south, hibernated individuals appear in spring. *Habitat* flowery areas to 6600 ft (2000 m). *Larvae* on nettles, sometimes on thistles.

Painted Lady *Description* male forewing 1 1/10 in (27-29mm); female similar. *Flight* from April onwards. *Habitat* flowery meadows and banks from lowlands to 6600 ft (2000 m). *Larvae* on thistles and nettles.

Small Tortoiseshell *Description* male forewing 9/10-1 in (22-25mm); female similar, slightly larger. *Flight* May onwards in several broods, hibernated individuals in March. *Habitat* flowery places to 7500 ft (2300 m). *Larvae* on nettles.

Comma *Description* male forewing 9/10 in (22-24mm); sexes similar. *Flight* two broods, June/August; hibernated individuals active March/April. *Habitat* flowery gardens, to 6000 ft (1800 m). *Larvae* on nettles, hops, willows, other trees.

Dark Green Fritillary *Description* male forewing 9/10-1 in (24-29mm); female similar, with ground colour slightly paler. *Flight* June-July. *Habitat* heaths, dune hollows, flowery meadows to treeline. *Larvae* on violets and Redshank.

Marbled White *Description* male forewing 9/10-1 in (23-26mm); female larger, hindwings beneath with pale yellow ground colour and yellow-brown marks. *Flight* June-July. *Habitat* grassy areas to 5250 ft (1600m). *Larvae* on grasses.

Woodland Grayling *Description* male forewing 1 1/4-1 1/2 in (33-38 mm); female larger, bands paler, more sharply defined. *Flight* July-August. *Habitat* among bushes and trees up to 3300 ft (1000 m). *Larvae* on grasses, especially Fog Grass.

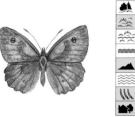

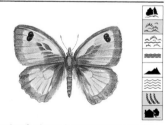

Gatekeeper *Description* male forewing 2/3-3/4 in (17-19mm); female larger, upperside ground colour brighter. *Flight* July-August. *Habitat* around brambles in lowlands and up to 3300 ft (1000 m). *Larvae* on meadow grasses and millets.

Southern Gatekeeper *Description* male forewing 3/5 in (15-16mm); female larger, lacks dark band in middle of forewing. *Flight* May-August, in a succession of broods. *Habitat* hot, rough, scrubby areas up to 5000 ft (1500 m). *Larvae* on grasses.

Speckled Wood *Description* male forewing ¾-⁹/₁₀in (19-22 mm); female similar. *Flight* March, with successive broods until October. *Habitat* woodland and shady areas to 4275 ft (1300 m). *Larvae* on Couch Grass and Creeping Wheat.

Smaller Copper *Description* male forewing ½--³/₅in (12-15 mm); female similar, often larger, with blunter forewing. *Flight* two or more broods from February-March. *Habitat* flowery areas to 6600 ft (2000 m). *Larvae* on docks, sorrels, and knot grass.

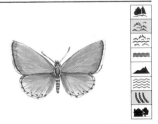 

Sooty Copper *Description* male forewing ³/₅in (14-16 mm); female slightly larger, forewings paler. *Flight* double-brooded, April/May and August/September. *Habitat* flowery meadows and waysides, up to 5000 ft (1500 m). *Larvae* on dock leaves.

Escher's Blue *Description* male forewing ⅔-¾in (17-19 mm); female uppersides brown, orange markings on sides. *Flight* late June-July. *Habitat* usually mountains up to 6600 ft (2000 m), sometimes in lowlands. *Larvae* on vetches.

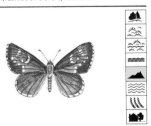  

Common Blue *Description* male forewing ³/₅-¾in (14-18 mm); female wings brown with blue flushes at bases. *Flight* two to three broods, from April onwards. *Habitat* open spaces, flowery meadows and waysides to 6600 ft (2000 m). *Larvae* on clovers, vetches.

Provence Chalk Hill Blue *Description* male forewing ³/₅-⅔in (16-18 mm); female wings brown. *Flight* double-brooded, April/May and September. *Habitat* grassy hillsides and banks up to 3000 ft (900 m). *Larvae* food plant unknown.

Carline Skipper *Description* male forewing ½in (13-14 mm); female with yellowish flush to uppersides. *Flight* July-August. *Habitat* mountain pastures, often in large gatherings on damp paths. *Larvae* on *Potentilla*.

Large Skipper *Description* male forewing ³/₅-⅔in (14-17 mm); female wings with series of pale spots. *Flight* June-August. *Habitat* fields and grassy banks up to 6000 ft (1800 m). *Larvae* on grasses and rushes.

Hornet Clearwing *Wingspan* 1⅖ in (36 mm). *Flight* May/June. *Habitat* lowlands, river banks, and waysides with poplars. *Larvae* feed in roots and lower trunks of poplars, taking three years to develop, before pupating under bark or in soil.

Six-spot Burnet *Wingspan* 1¼-1⅖ in (33-36 mm). *Flight* July/August. *Habitat* hillsides, cliffs, grassland, in chalky areas, also on sand-dunes. *Larvae* on clover, trefoils, and vetches, completing growth and pupating in spring.

Nine-spotted Syntomid Moth *Wingspan* 1⅓-1⅗ in (35-40 mm). *Flight* June-August. *Habitat* woodland margins, warm, flowery slopes, and hillsides, often on Marjoram flowers. *Larvae* on various herbaceous plants.

Red Underwing *Wingspan* 2½-3 in (65-75 mm). *Flight* July-October. *Habitat* urban parks, moist deciduous woodlands in the north, often near water. *Larvae* on various kinds of poplars and willows.

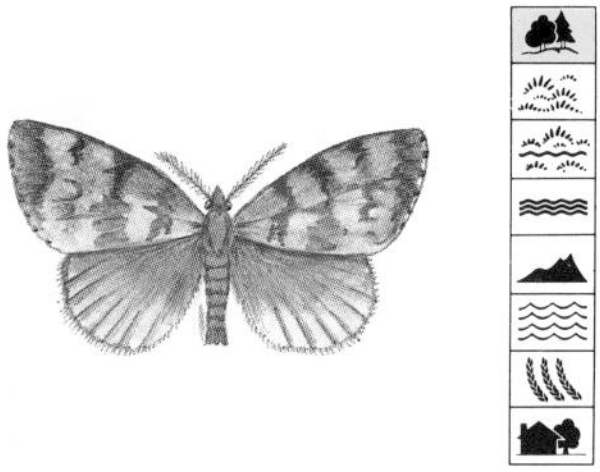

Gypsy Moth *Wingspan* male, 1⅖-1⅗ in (36-40 mm), female 2⅖-2⅔ in (68-72 mm); female with pale wings, antennae not feathery. *Flight* June-August. *Habitat* woodland; males fly by day in erratic zig-zag, females cumbersome. *Larvae* major pest of trees.

Emperor Moth *Wingspan* 1⅗-2⅓ in (40-60 mm); females without feathery antennae, ground colour of wings grey rather than orange-brown. *Flight* April/May. *Habitat* lowlands, mountains to 6600 ft (2000 m). *Larvae* on Blackthorn, willows, Bilberry.

Death's Head Hawkmoth *Wingspan* 3⅒-4¾ in (80-120 mm). *Flight* May/June, immigrant from Africa and south-west Asia. *Habitat* cultivated areas in lowlands. *Larvae* on potato family: potatoes, Woody Nightshade, Thorn-apple.

Eyed Hawkmoth *Wingspan* 2¾-3⅒ in (70-80 mm). *Flight* May-July. *Habitat* lowlands, mountains up to 6600 ft (2000 m), urban parks; nocturnal. *Larvae* on poplars and willows, sometimes fruit trees.

Convolvulus Hawkmoth *Wingspan* 3¹⁄₁₀-4¾ in (80-120 mm). *Flight* May-July, immigrant from Africa and Asia. *Habitat* flowery areas, feeding at tubular flowers such as phlox, with 4-in (10-cm)-long proboscis. *Larvae* on bindweeds.

Spurge Hawkmoth *Wingspan* 2¼-3 in (55-75 mm). *Flight* May-August. *Habitat* waste areas, marginal land, dry, scrubby waysides. *Larvae* on various kinds of spurge.

Oleander Hawkmoth *Wingspan* 3½-5¹⁄₁₀ in (90-130 mm). *Flight* July-September. *Habitat* cultivated and woody areas, urban parks, and gardens. *Larvae* on Oleander and Periwinkle.

Bedstraw Hawkmoth *Wingspan* 2¹⁄₃-3¹⁄₁₀ in (60-80 mm). *Flight* May-September, in one or two generations. *Habitat* lowlands, mountains to 6600 ft (2000 m), flowery hillsides, woodland glades in daytime. *Larvae* on bedstraw and willowherb.

Mediterranean Hawkmoth *Wingspan* 3¹⁄₃-4 in (85-100 mm). *Flight* May-September. *Habitat* dry hillsides, scrubby waysides, margins of open woodlands. *Larvae* on various kinds of spurge.

Striped Hawkmoth *Wingspan* 2¹⁄₃-3¹⁄₁₀ in (60-80 mm). *Flight* double brooded, May/June, August/September. *Habitat* very varied, almost everywhere, often at flowers of phlox in early evenings. *Larvae* on willowherb and bedstraw.

Silver-striped Hawkmoth *Wingspan* 2¾-3¹⁄₁₀ in (70-80 mm). *Flight* double brooded, May-September, frequently migrates north. *Habitat* almost everywhere. *Larvae* on grapevines, bedstraw, fuchsias, Virginia Creeper, Cotton.

Large Elephant Hawkmoth *Wingspan* 1¾-2¹⁄₃ in (45-60 mm). *Flight* May-July, sometimes a second generation, August. *Habitat* from lowlands to mountains up to 5000 ft (1500 m). *Larvae* on willowherbs and bedstraws.

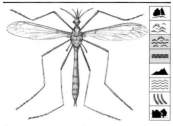

Great Cranefly *Wingspan* 2½ in (65 mm). *Season* spring and summer. *Habitat* damp, marshy areas, stream- and lakesides, ditches. *Larvae* semiaquatic, in saturated margins of ponds, streams, or, sometimes living under water.

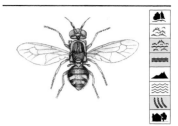

Soldier Fly *Wingspan* ⅗-½ in (10-12 mm). *Season* summer. *Habitat* damp meadows, ditches, waterside vegetation, often seen on umbellifer flowers. *Larvae* in ponds, ditches, preying on small water animals, including insects.

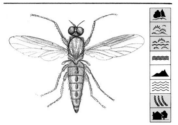

Snipe Fly *Wingspan* 1-1¹⁄₁₀ in (26-28 mm). *Season* summer-early autumn. *Habitat* hedgerows, meadows, woodland edges, often resting head down on treetrunks. *Larvae* carnivorous, living in leaf litter, under bark of fallen trees.

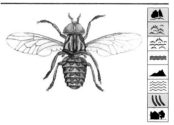

Horsefly *Wingspan* 1¹⁄₁₀-1⅕ in (27-30 mm). *Season* May-September. *Habitat* fields, open woodlands, females sucking blood of livestock; males nectar-feeders. *Larvae* carnivorous, preying on worms, insect larvae in soil, dead wood.

Bee-fly *Wingspan* ⅘-⁹⁄₁₀ in (20-22 mm). *Season* June-August. *Habitat* dry, sandy areas, heaths, sand-dunes, often seen resting on bare sand. *Larvae* parasites of caterpillars.

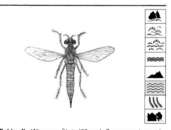

Robberfly *Wingspan* ⁹⁄₁₀ in (22 mm). *Season* spring and summer. *Habitat* dry sandy areas in coastal regions, especially sand-dunes, where the flies prey on other insects. *Larvae* feed on decaying vegetable matter in soil, sand.

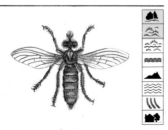

Robberfly *Wingspan* ⁹⁄₁₀ in (21-23 mm). *Season* late spring-summer. *Habitat* woodlands, sunny clearings, meadows, leaping on insect prey from points such as treestumps, rocks. *Larvae* in soil, feeding on humus and other decaying matter.

Slow Flower Fly *Wingspan* 1¹⁄₁₀-1⅕ in (28-30 mm). *Season* spring-summer. *Habitat* hot, dry, stony, and sandy places where often seen sipping nectar from flowers while hovering. *Larvae* possibly parasites of beetle larvae.

Dronefly *Wingspan* 1-1¹⁄₁₀ in (26-29 mm). *Season* early spring to autumn. *Habitat* flowers in waysides, woodlands, hedgebanks, gardens, farmyards, closely resembling Honeybee. *Larvae* in stagnant water, called 'rat-tailed maggots'.

Hoverfly *Wingspan* ²⁄₃-⁹⁄₁₀ in (17-23 mm). *Season* April-September. *Habitat* gardens, urban wasteland, hedgerows, often seen at umbelliferous flowers and, in September, on asters. *Larvae* in stagnant and polluted water.

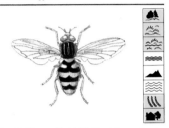

Hoverfly *Wingspan* ⁹⁄₁₀-1 in (24-26 mm). *Season* March-November. *Habitat* varied, gardens, hedgerows, wasteground, woodland clearings, cultivated areas, often at umbellifer flowers. *Larvae* live on plants, where they eat aphids.

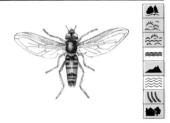

Hoverfly *Wingspan* ¹⁄₃-¹⁄₂ in (8-13 mm). *Season* January-December. *Habitat* almost everywhere, often in vast numbers, usually seen on umbellifer flowers; migratory; vast swarms following 'aphid years'. *Larvae* on plants, feeding on aphids.

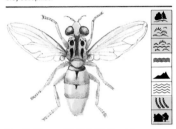

Hoverfly *Wingspan* 1³⁄₅-1³⁄₄ in (40-44 mm). *Season* May-October. *Habitat* flowery meadows, hedgerows, woodland glades, and waysides, often on umbellifers, or ivy flowers. *Larvae* live as scavengers in nests of social wasps.

Hoverfly *Wingspan* 1¹⁄₁₀-1¹⁄₄ in (28-33 mm). *Season* June-September. *Habitat* flower-rich meadows, hillsides and woodlands. *Larvae* live as scavengers in Hornet nests.

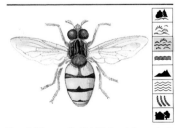

Hoverfly *Wingspan* 1¹⁄₂-1³⁄₅ in (39-41 mm). *Season* April-September. *Habitat* flower-rich areas, often near damp or marshy ground; at flowers of umbels, mint. *Larvae* feeding on damp, rotting plant material and other decaying organic matter.

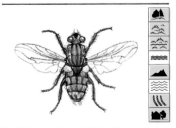

Fleshfly *Wingspan* ⁹⁄₁₀-1 in (23-25 mm). *Season* March-November. *Habitat* varied, almost everywhere, including towns; at umbels and other flowers, attracted to rotting meat. *Larvae* female lays small larvae on meat, dead animals.

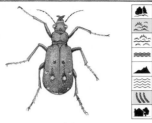

Field Tiger Beetle *Length* ⅖-⅗ in (10.5-14.5 mm). *Season* April-September. *Habitat* dry, sandy areas, dry fields with bare earth; runs rapidly, flies readily, preys on insects. *Larvae* live in short burrows, darting out to catch insect prey.

Hybrid Tiger Beetle *Length* ½-⅗ in (11.5-15.5 mm). *Season* April-October. *Habitat* sandy areas, especially coastal dunes, but often inland, up to 6600 ft (2000 m); preys on insects, flies readily. *Larvae* in short burrows, darting out to catch insect prey.

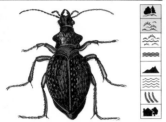

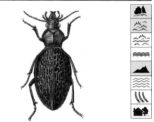

Giant Ground Beetle *Length* 1½-2⅓ in (40-60 mm). *Season* spring/summer. *Habitat* open, dry woodland, hillsides, feeding on snails. *Larvae* same habits as adults.

Coriaceous Ground Beetle *Length* 1⅕-1⅗ in (30-40 mm). *Season* spring-autumn, hibernating through winter; adults may live 2-3 years. *Habitat* varied, from lowlands to mountains, under stones during day. *Larvae* prey on other insects.

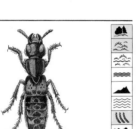

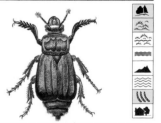

Grey-haired Rove Beetle *Length* ⅗-1 in (15-25 mm). *Season* spring-autumn. *Habitat* decomposing matter, especially bodies of dead animals, in a wide variety of situations. *Larvae* feed on carrion.

Great Burying Beetle *Length* ⅔-1 in (18-26 mm). *Season* spring-autumn. *Habitat* in dead bodies and rotting fungi in a wide range of situations; adults bury small mammals as future food for their offspring. *Larvae* feeding in carrion.

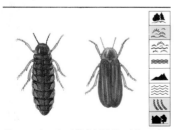

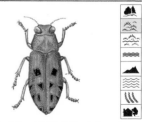

Glowworm *Length* male ⅖-½ in (10-12 mm), female ⅗-⅘ in (15-20 mm). *Season* June-September. *Habitat* chalky areas; prey on snails; female resembles larva, is flightless, produces green light on warm evenings to attract males. *Larvae* eat snails.

Jewel Beetle *Length* ¼-½ in (6-12 mm). *Season* June-August. *Habitat* open grassland, flying around Juniper trees. *Larvae* feed on Juniper, under the bark.

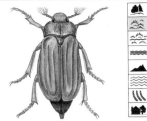

Common Cockchafer or Maybug *Length* ⅘-1⅕ in (20-30 mm). *Season* May-June. *Habitat* open countryside with scattered trees, up to 1000 m. *Larvae* feed at the roots of plants

European Rhinoceros Beetle *Length* ⅘-1⅗ in (20-40 mm). *Season* April-July; female with smaller horn than male. *Habitat* leaf mould, humus, in wooded areas. *Larvae* in rotting wood.

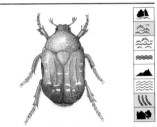

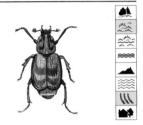

Rose Chafer *Length* ⅗-⅘ in (14-20 mm). *Season* April-September. *Habitat* open country with flowery areas, waysides, usually sitting on flowers; takes to flight readily. *Larvae* feed on rotting wood and humus.

Striped Chafer *Length* male, ¼-⅖ in (6-10 mm), female, including tail spine, ½-⅗ in (12-14 mm); female with fainter pale stripes and long tail spine. *Season* May/June. *Habitat* on flowers in rich meadows. *Larvae* feed in rotting wood.

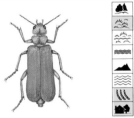

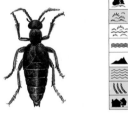

Spanish Fly *Length* ⅓-⅘ in (9-21 mm). *Season* spring-summer. *Habitat* flowery meadows; beetles once sold as an aphrodisiac, contain the toxin cantharadin; BLISTERING IF HANDLED. *Larvae* parasites of grasshopper eggs.

Oil Beetle *Length* ⅖-1⅓ in (11-35 mm). *Season* late spring-summer. *Habitat* low-lying, flat country, especially in areas with a light or sandy soil. *Larvae* live as parasites inside the nest cells of solitary bees, eating the egg and stored food.

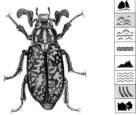

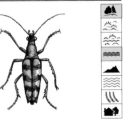

Large Chafer *Length* 1-1⅖ in (25-36 mm). *Season* late spring-early summer. *Habitat* lowland areas, including cultivated land; adults fly in evening. *Larvae* carnivorous, preying on the larvae of other beetles, development taking 3-4 years.

Striped Longhorn Beetle *Length* ⅖-⅘ in (11-19 mm). *Season* July-August. *Habitat* open woodland, wooded river banks, often on flowers of umbels or tree trunks, logs. *Larvae* feed on the wood of several tree species, but especially willows.

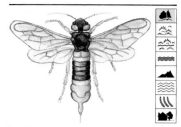

Great Woodwasp or Horntail *Wingspan* 1¾-2¼ in (44-55 mm); males lack egg-laying tube at rear. *Season* summer. *Habitat* coniferous woods; females use stiff egg depositor to drill hole and lay egg in treetrunk. *Larvae* in dead or dying firs.

Willow Sawfly *Wingspan* ³⁄₅ in (14-15 mm). *Season* summer. *Habitat* riverside vegetation, damp, marshy areas with willows; females lay eggs in willow leaves. *Larvae* develop in pink galls induced by presence of egg in willow leaves.

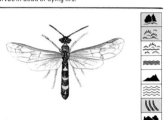

Wheat Stem-borer *Wingspan* ½ in (12-13 mm). *Season* late spring-summer. *Habitat* grasslands, grassy areas in woodland rides, wheat fields. *Larvae* live in grass stems, including wheat and are a pest of cereal crops.

Long-tailed Ichneumon Wasp *Wingspan* 1½-1¾ in (38-45 mm); female with egg-laying tube, absent in males. *Season* summer. *Habitat* coniferous woods; females drill hole with egg-laying tube, lay egg into timber. *Larvae* eat Great Woodwasp larvae.

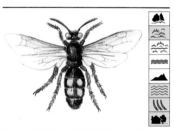

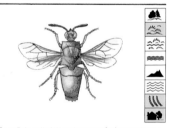

Large Scolia *Wingspan* 1⅓-2⅓ in (35-60 mm). *Season* early summer-autumn. *Habitat* dry, open, stony country, both sexes often on flowers, especially umbels. *Larvae* external parasites of chafer beetle larvae.

Great Ruby-tailed Wasp *Wingspan* ⅔-⅘ in (17-20 mm). *Season* late spring-summer. *Habitat* warm, dry, and usually stony fields and hillsides, often at flowers. *Larvae* parasitize the larvae of wasps and bees which build exposed mud nests.

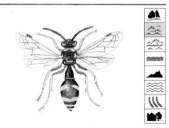

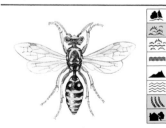

Heath Potter Wasp *Wingspan* ³⁄₅-⅘ in (16-20 mm). *Season* summer. *Habitat* dry, open, areas and heaths with heather; solitary females build mud nest suspended from heather twig. *Larvae* feed on caterpillar provided by female wasp.

French Polistes *Wingspan* ⁹⁄₁₀-1 in (23-26 mm). *Season* spring-summer. *Habitat* open country; founding female (queen) builds paper nest from branch, female offspring act as non-reproductive workers. *Larvae* eat chewed insect prey provided by workers.

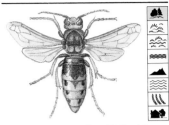

Western Hornet *Wingspan* 1⅓-2 in (35-50 mm). *Season* spring-autumn. *Habitat* open woodland, parkland with mature trees; colonies build paper nests in hollow trees. *Larvae* feed on chewed insect prey caught by workers.

Yellow Spider-hunting Wasp *Wingspan* 1⅔-1⁹⁄₁₀ in (43-48 mm). *Season* summer. *Habitat* hot, dry, sandy areas, dunes, hillsides; females store paralyzed spiders in nest in ground. *Larvae* each feeds on a single spider collected by mother wasp.

Red Spider-hunting Wasp *Wingspan* ⅔-⁹⁄₁₀ in (18-22 mm). *Season* late spring-summer. *Habitat* dry, sandy areas on chalk or sand, especially dunes near sea; heaths; female paralyzes spider with sting. *Larva* feeds on spider caught by female.

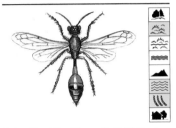

Solitary Digger Wasp *Wingspan* ⁹⁄₁₀-1 in (22-25 mm). *Season* spring-summer. *Habitat* dry, sandy areas; open, dry grasslands; females provision each nest with several caterpillars. *Larvae* live in nest in ground, eat prey captured by female.

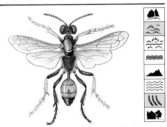

Bush Cricket-hunting Wasp *Wingspan* 1⅓-1⅗ in (35-40 mm). *Season* spring-summer. *Habitat* dry, stony wastes and hillsides; females provision nest with paralyzed bush crickets. *Larvae* in nest in ground, one per nest, eat bush crickets.

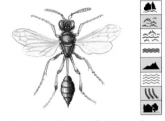

Mud-dauber Wasp *Wingspan* 1-1⅕ (25-30 mm). *Season* spring-summer. *Habitat* dry, rocky areas; female builds exposed mud nest of several cells, provisions each cell with several spiders and lays egg in it. *Larvae* eat spiders.

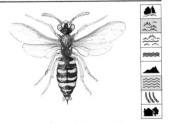

Sand Wasp *Wingspan* 1-1⅕ (25-30 mm). *Season* summer. *Habitat* dry, sandy areas; females collect flies, sting and paralyze them, provide them as food for larvae in nest dug in sand; very rapid, darting flight. *Larvae* eat flies.

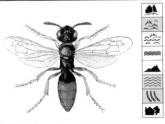

Bee Wolf *Wingspan* ⅘-1⅕ (20-30 mm). *Season* summer. *Habitat* dry sandy or stony areas with exposures of clay soil; female provisions underground nest with captured bees, including Honeybees. *Larvae* feed on bees.

55

Great Digger Bee *Wingspan* 1-1⅕ (25-30 mm). *Season* spring-summer. *Habitat* open country, marginal land; nests dug in ground by single females, which collect pollen and nectar from wide range of flowers. *Larvae* eat pollen.

Shrub Mason Bee *Wingspan* 9/10-1 1/10 in (23-28 mm). *Season* spring. *Habitat* open, stony countryside; females build exposed mud nests on branches, shrubs, or rocks, collect pollen from vetches, bugloss flowers. *Larvae* eat pollen/nectar.

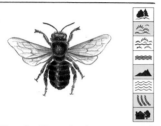

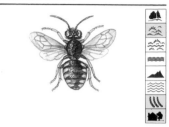

Wall Mason Bee *Wingspan* 9/10-1 1/10 in (22-27 mm). *Season* spring-summer. *Habitat* dry, open, stony, and rocky areas; females build exposed mud nests on rocks, stones, walls, ancient monuments. *Larvae* eat pollen/nectar mixture.

Common Carder Bee *Wingspan* ⅘ in (19-21 mm). *Season* July-September. *Habitat* flowery areas, gardens, scrubby hillsides; females line nests in old beetle borings in wood, with cottony down collected from hairy leaves. *Larvae* eat nectar/pollen.

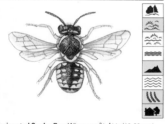

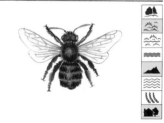

Variegated Carder Bee *Wingspan* ⅗-⅘ in (16-20 mm). *Season* summer. *Habitat* dry, scrubby hillsides, sandy wastes; females nest in beetle borings in dead wood or hollow plant stems, lining them with plant hairs. *Larvae* eat pollen/nectar mixture.

Black Anthophora *Wingspan* ⅔-⅘ in (17-19 mm); female pale brown rather than black in south. *Season* spring. *Habitat* rocky areas with cliffs; females nest in vertical cliff faces, old walls; forage at tubular flowers. *Larvae* eat pollen/nectar.

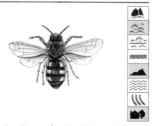

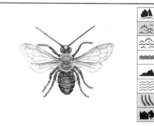

Cuckoo Bee *Wingspan* 9/10-1 1/10 in (24-27 mm). *Season* spring. *Habitat* rocky areas with cliffs; females enter nests of anthophora bees and lay eggs there. *Larvae* eat food store after killing host egg or young larva.

Long-horned Bee *Wingspan* 9/10-1 in (22-25 mm); females lack long antennae, have white hairs at side of abdomen. *Habitat* flowery meadows. *Larvae* eat pollen/nectar mixture stored by females.

Violet Carpenter Bee *Wingspan* 1¾-2 in (45-50 mm).
Season spring-summer. *Habitat* open country, scrubby
areas; females bore in solid wood or use hollow stems;
nest partitioned with wood fragments. *Larvae* eat
pollen/nectar mixture.

Buff-tailed Bumblebee *Wingspan* 1¹⁄₁₀-1²⁄₃ in (28-
42 mm); queens larger than workers. *Season* spring-
early autumn. *Habitat* most kinds of countryside to
6000 ft (1800 m); queen founds nest in old rodent nest.
Larvae reared in wax cells.

Early Bumblebee *Wingspan* ⅘-1¼ in (20-32 mm);
queens slightly larger than workers. *Season* spring-
autumn. *Habitat* lowlands, mountains up to 3300 ft
(1000 m); nests in grass tussocks, old birds' nests, earth
banks. *Larvae* reared in wax cells.

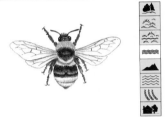

Ginger Bumblebee *Wingspan* ⅗-1¼ in (16-32 mm);
variable, some individuals very dark. *Season* spring-
autumn. *Habitat* lowland areas, flowery meadows,
gardens; nests in grass tussocks, old birds' nests.
Larvae reared in wax cells.

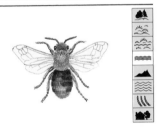

Garden Bumblebee *Wingspan* 1⅕-1½ in (30-39 mm).
Season spring-summer. *Habitat* gardens, woodland,
hedgerows; long tongue enables bees to probe deep
flowers; nests in holes in earth banks, mouse nests.
Larvae reared in wax cells.

Red-tailed Bumblebee *Wingspan* ⁹⁄₁₀-1⅗ in (22-40 mm).
Season spring-summer. *Habitat* scrubby areas,
hedgerows, waste ground, gardens; nests in old rodent
burrows, under rocks and garden refuse. *Larvae* reared
in wax cells.

Vestal Cuckoo Bee *Wingspan* 1⅖-1½ in (35.5-39 mm).
Season early summer-autumn. *Habitat* most kinds of
countryside, including mountains up to 6000 ft (1800 m);
females lay eggs in nests of Buff-tailed Bumblebee.
Larvae reared by workers of host.

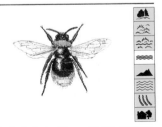

Bohemian Cuckoobee *Wingspan* 1¼-1½ in (32-37 mm).
Season early summer-autumn. *Habitat* open
countryside, hedgerows, woodland margins; females
lay eggs in nests of another bumblebee species. *Larvae*
reared by workers of host.

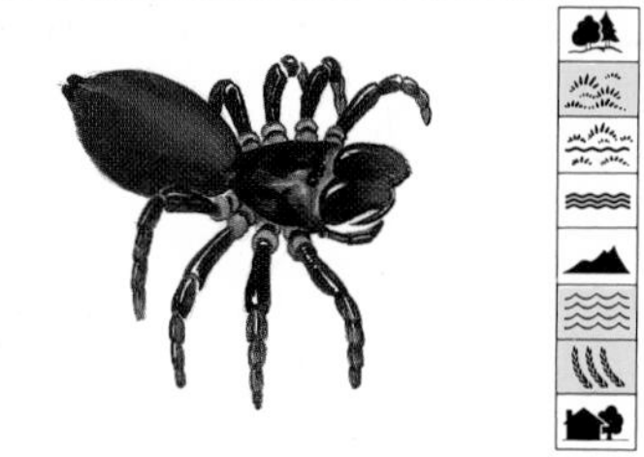

Purse-web Spider *Length* male ¼-⅓ in (7-9 mm), female ⅖-⅗ in (10-15 mm). *Habitat* dry, sandy areas; silk-lined nest tube excavated under low plants, often in mounds of Yellow Meadow Ant. *Season* older females all year, otherwise, mainly autumn.

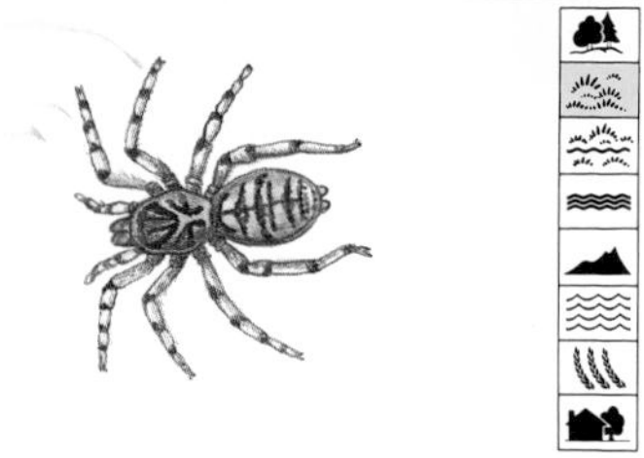

European Trap-door Spider *Length* male ⅖ in (11 mm), female ⅗-⅘ in (15-20 mm). *Habitat* dry, sandy areas, unbranched, silk-lined tunnel 4¾-5 in (12-13 cm) deep, lid camouflaged with moss and other vegetation. *Season* all year.

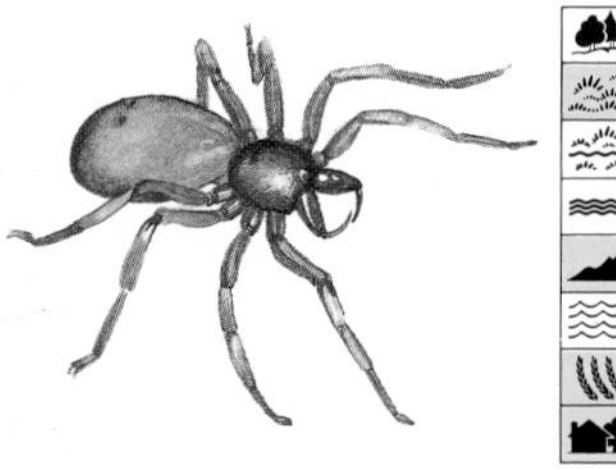

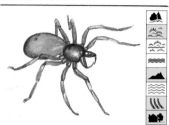

Woodlouse-hunting Spider *Length* male about ⅖ in (10 mm), female about ½ in (12 mm). *Habitat* under stones and logs in warm, dry places, where it preys on woodlice. *Season* all year.

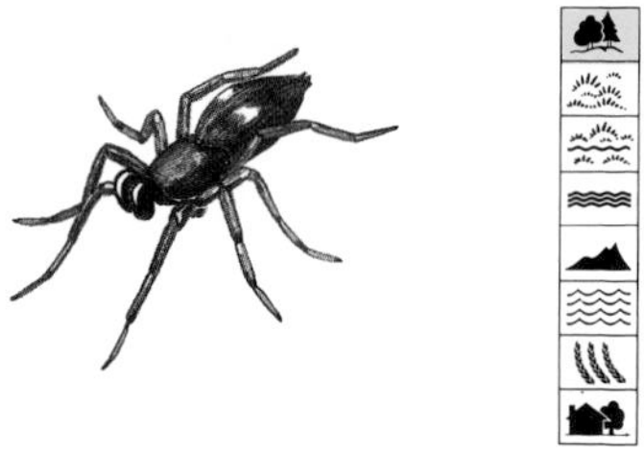

Southern Pinewood Spider *Length* male ⅒ in (3 mm), female ⅒ in (3.5 mm). *Habitat* among stones in pinewoods; feeds on ants, biting at bases of antennae and waiting for venom to take effect; prey often dragged to retreat. *Season* spring.

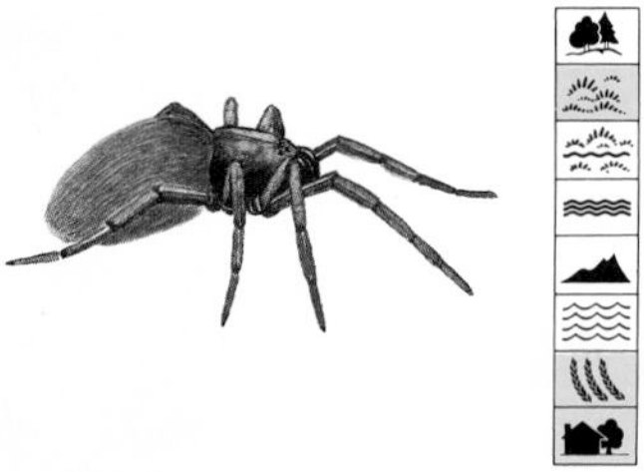

Mouse Spider *Length* male ⅖-½ in (10-13 mm), female ⅔-⅘ in (18-19 mm). *Habitat* under stones and in dry tussocks of grass; mainly a nocturnal hunter, preying on insects, aggressive towards other spiders. *Season* mainly spring.

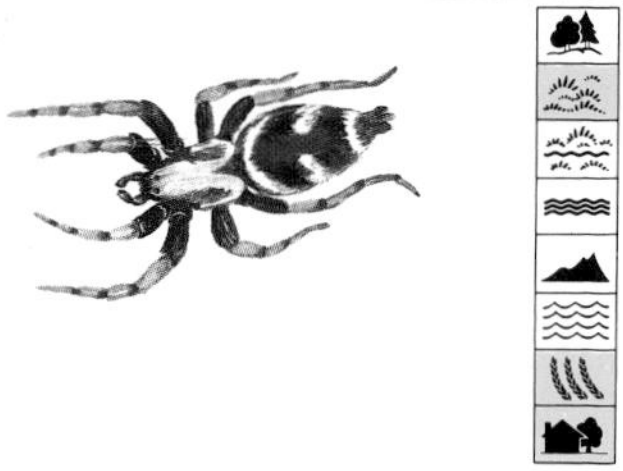

Pale-barred Spider *Length* male about ¼ in (6 mm), female about ⅓ in (8 mm). *Habitat* in debris and under stones in dry, sandy places; less nocturnal than many spiders. *Season* spring and summer.

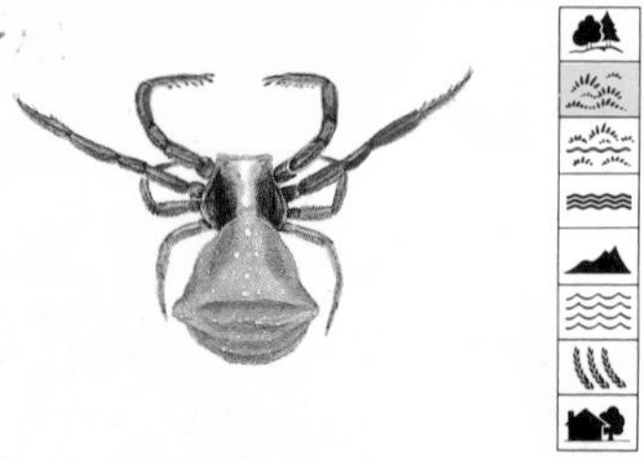

Heath Crab Spider *Length* male ⅒ in (3 mm), female ¼ in (7 mm); male body dark brown, conspicuous female seen most frequently. *Habitat* flowers, especially heather, where it lies in wait for flower-visiting insects. *Season* early-midsummer.

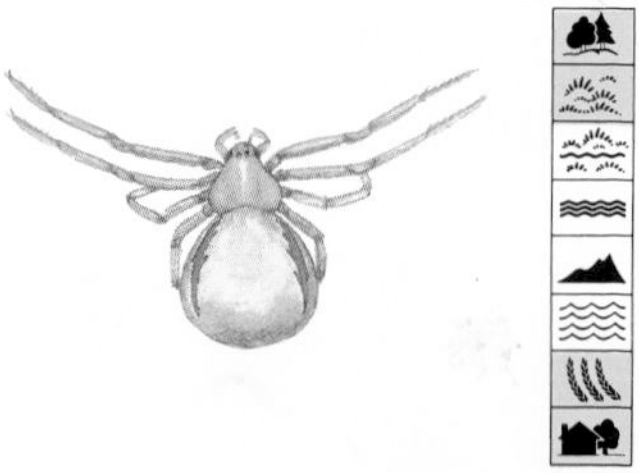

Common Crab Spider *Length* male ⅙ in (4 mm), female ⅖ in (10 mm); male body dark brown, female's variable, changes with floral background colour. *Habitat* usually white or yellow flowers. *Season* early and midsummer.

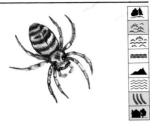

Common Jumping Spider *Length* male about ⅕ in (5 mm), female about ¼ in (6 mm). *Habitat* rocks, stones, wood sheds, fences, gardens; stalks insect prey using eyes that are highly sensitive to any movement. *Season* early-late summer.

Orange Jumping Spider *Length* ¼-½ in (7-12 mm); female with central black stripe flanked by light brown, unlike bright orange of male. *Habitat* sometimes low bushes, otherwise mainly among rocks and stones. *Season* summer.

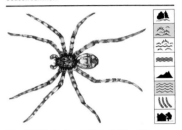

Heath Wolf Spider *Length* male ½ in (12 mm), female ⅗ in (15 mm). *Habitat* sandy, heathy places, where female digs deep, silk-lined burrow, in which she guards egg sac. *Season* early-midsummer.

Dune Wolf Spider *Length* ⅓ in (male 8.5 mm), female ⅓ in (8 mm). *Habitat* sandy places, both inland and coastal; excavates burrow, though both sexes often seen running over sand surface. *Season* autumn, spring, early summer.

European True Tarantula *Length* ⅖-⅔ in (10-18 mm). *Habitat* dry, stony hillsides with Thyme; spiders live in burrows from which they leap out and capture insects, especially grasshoppers. *Season* spring-summer.

Slim Wolf Spider *Length* male ⅖-½ in (10-12 mm), female ½-⅗ in (12-15 mm). *Habitat* woods, heaths, lush hedgerows and gardens, female often seen carrying white egg sac. *Season* early summer.

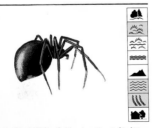

European Black Widow Spider. *Length* male ¹⁄₁₀-⅕ in (3-5 mm), female ⅓-½ in (8-12 mm). *Bite* female's VERY POISONOUS causing intense pain. *Habitat* low vegetation in dry areas, small web strung close to ground. *Season* spring-summer.

Golden Orb Web Spider *Length* male ⅙ in (4 mm), female ⅗ in (15 mm); male with elongate abdomen, with two vague brown stripes. *Habitat* grassy areas, low vegetation, large web up to 1⅕ in (30 cm) across. *Season* spring-early autumn.

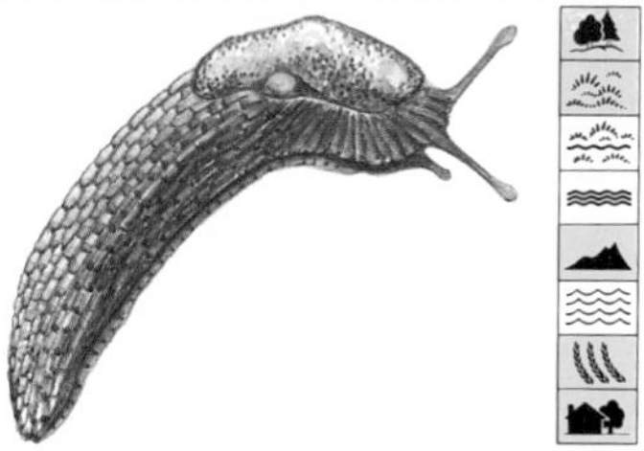

Large Black Slug *Length* (extended) 4-6 in (10-15 cm), sometimes 8 in (20 cm). *Habitat* woods, grasslands, moors, gardens, up to 6000 ft (1800 m); hunches up when touched and rocks from side to side.

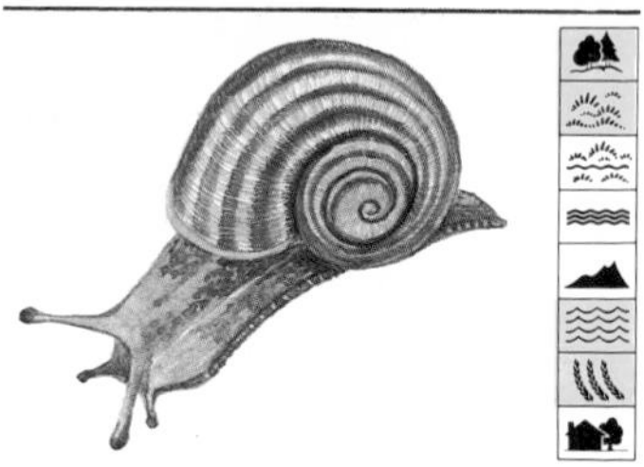

Grove Snail *Shell* height ½-9/10 in (12-22 mm), width ⅔-1 in (18-25 mm). *Habitat* very varied, ranging from sand-dunes and grasslands to scrub, hedgerows, and woodlands, up to 4000 ft (1200 m) in the Alps and 6000 ft (1800 m) in the Pyrénées.

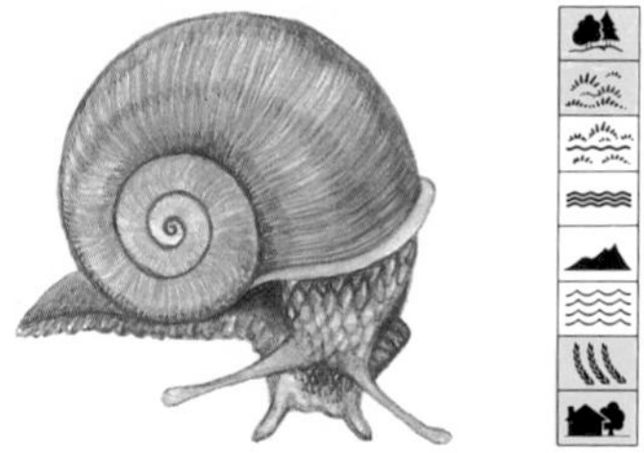

Roman Snail *Shell* height 1⅕-2 in (30-50 mm), width 1¼-2 in (32-50 mm). *Habitat* tall herbage, hedges, and woodland in chalk and limestone areas; often a pest in vineyards, although 'cultivated' as food in some areas.

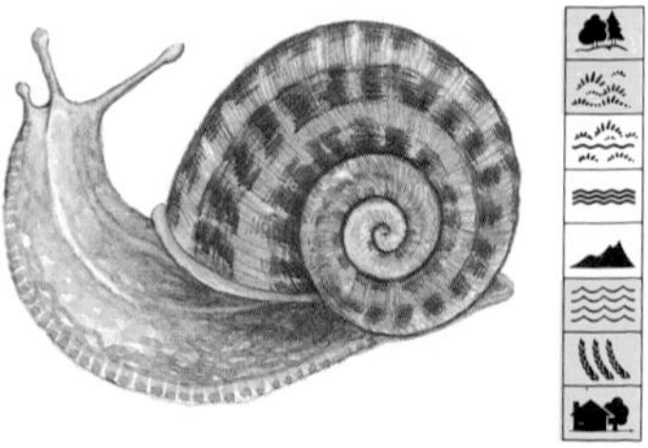

Garden Snail *Shell* height 1-1⅓ in (25-35 mm), width 1-1⅗ in (25-40 mm). *Habitat* varied, banks, ivy-covered walls, cliffs, quarries, hedges, evergreen shrubs in gardens, dunes, woods, individuals returning to fixed home after feeding trips.

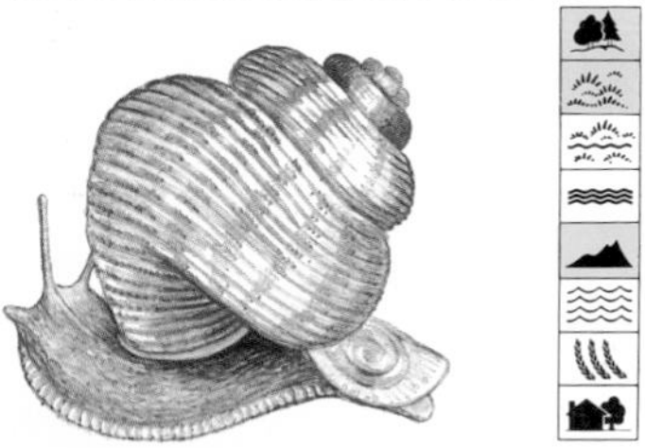

Round-mouthed Snail *Shell* height ½-⅗ in (13-16 mm), width ⅓-½ in (9-12 mm). *Habitat* chalky areas with dry, friable soil in which it burrows; hedgebanks, open woodland, screes.

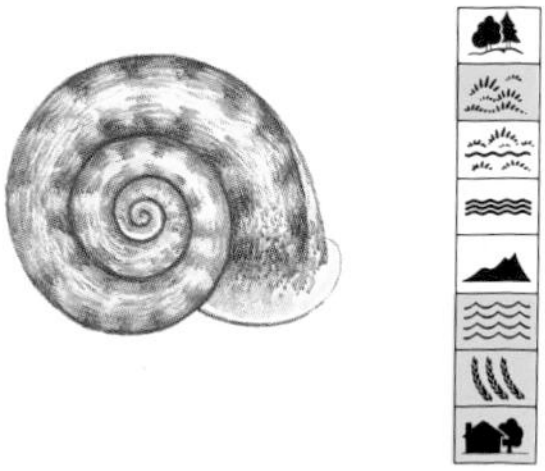

Common Mediterranean Snail *Shell* height ⅗-1 1/10 in (14-27 mm), width 9/10-1⅕ (22-30 mm). *Habitat* dry, grassy places, fields, waysides, gardens, Olive groves, vineyards, and hedgerows.

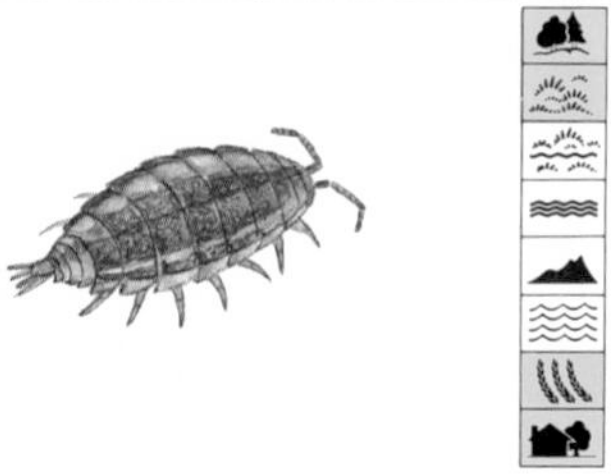

Woodlouse *Length* ¼-½ in (6-12 mm). *Habitat* varied, includes grassland, hedgerows, waysides, woodland edges, gardens, less often in woodland.

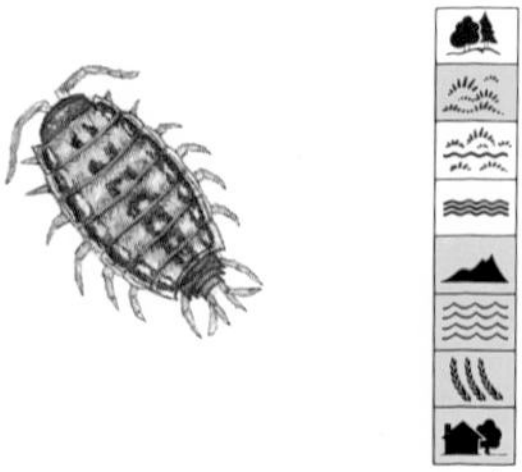

Downland Woodlouse *Length* ⅖-⅗ in (10-16 mm). *Habitat* areas with dry, well-drained soils, usually chalk downlands, but also hedgerows, gardens, and coastal regions, especially sand-dunes.

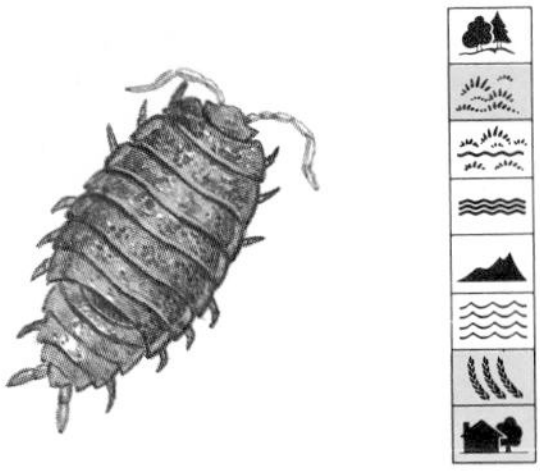

Wall Woodlouse *Length* $\frac{2}{5}$-$\frac{2}{3}$ in (11-18 mm). *Habitat* prefers drier places than most other woodlice, such as old tumbledown walls and ruins, dry terraces, and often comes into houses.

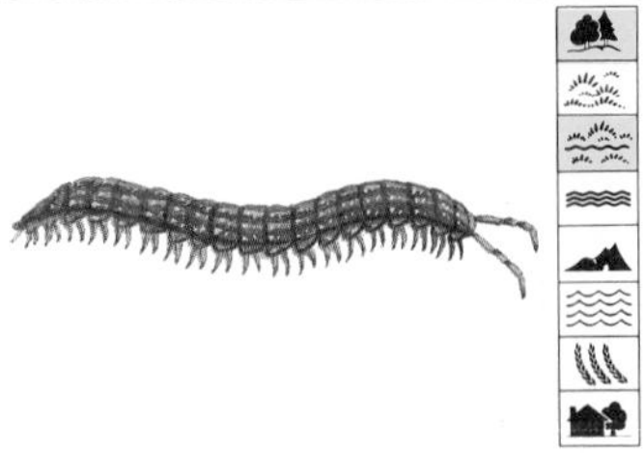

Flat-backed Millipede *Length* $\frac{2}{3}$-1 in (17-25 mm). *Habitat* prefers damp places, under stones, cracks in soil, where it feeds on the roots of plants.

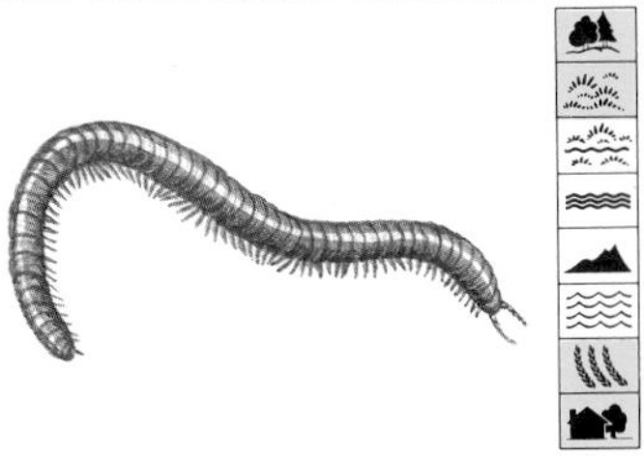

Swift-footed Millipede *Length* $\frac{4}{5}$-2 in (19-50 mm). *Habitat* in leaf litter in woodland, under bark of dead trees, chalk grassland, old walls; climbs walls and tree trunks at night to feed on algae; often comes into houses.

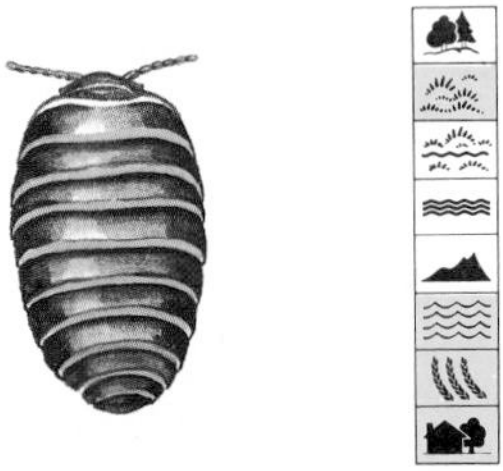

Pill Millipede *Length* $\frac{2}{3}$-$\frac{4}{5}$ in (17-20 mm). *Habitat* among vegetation in a variety of situations, including dry areas such as sand-dunes and heaths; when disturbed, rolls up into a ball for protection.

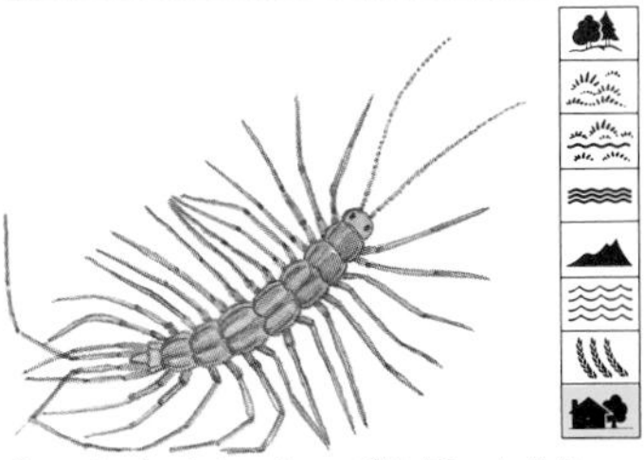

House Centipede *Length* up to 1$\frac{1}{5}$ in (30 mm). *Habitat* usually near buildings, where it preys on insects and other small animals; extremely fast runner, especially at night, when disturbed by light.

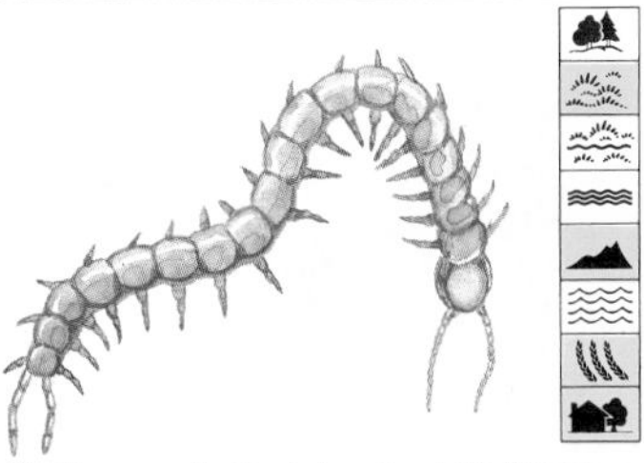

Mediterranean Centipede *Length* up to 1 in (25 mm). *Habitat* in rock crevices, between boulders, often in buildings, where it preys on insects and other small animals, even small lizards. In the south.

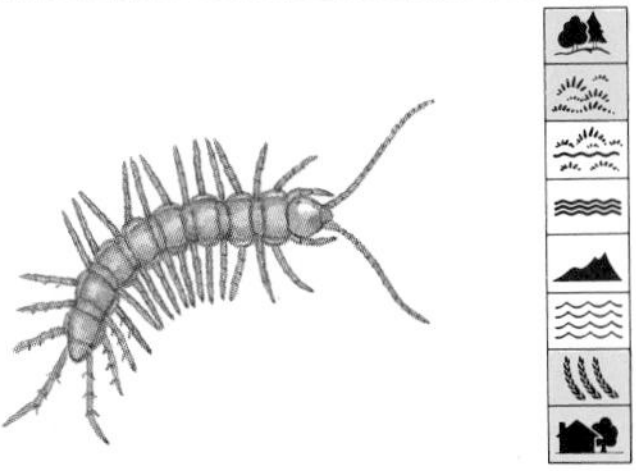

Stone-dwelling Centipede *Length* $\frac{2}{3}$-1$\frac{1}{5}$ (18-30 mm). *Habitat* varied, open woodland, under bark of dead trees, under logs, open country under stones, gardens, houses; feeds on insects, slugs, and earthworms. BITES IF HANDLED.

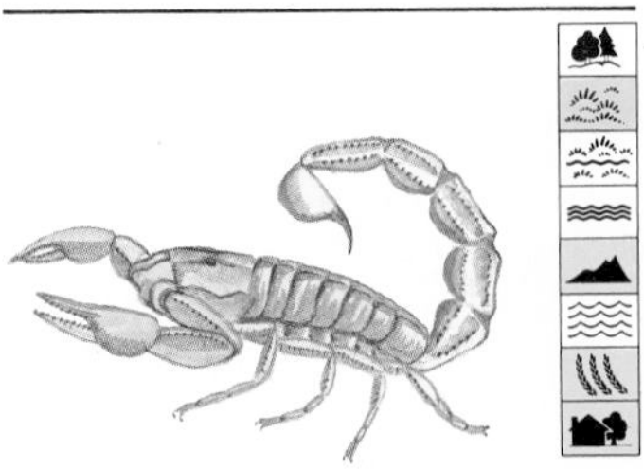

Mediterranean Scorpion *Length* up to 1$\frac{1}{3}$ in (35 mm). *Habitat* under stones in dry areas, coming out at dusk and throughout night to feed on insects and other small animals, which it kills with venomous sting. PAINFUL STING IF HANDLED.

Common Seal *Length* up to 63 in (160 cm), sexes similar. *Call* usually silent, but will sometimes bark at night. *Habitat* around flat coastline with rocks or sand; occasionally migrate up large rivers; live in small groups.

Grey Seal *Length* up to 118 in (300 cm), female smaller. *Colour* variable; distinguish from Common Seal by size and longer muzzle. *Call* loud wails, and moans, particularly during mating season. *Habitat* on rocky coasts and islands.

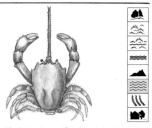

Masked Crab *Length* up to 1½ in (4 cm). *Shell* oval. Male front legs much longer than female's, with smaller pincers. *Habitat* on lower shore, where it burrows into sand.

Common Shore Crab *Length* up to 2¼ in (6 cm). *Shell* variable, green to mottled black; juveniles sandy coloured. *Habitat* middle to lower shore and water's edge; also saltmarsh.

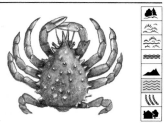

Spiny Spider Crab *Length* up to 10 in (25 cm). *Shell* pear shaped, encrusted with knobs and spines. Legs very hairy. *Habitat* on sandy bottoms to depth of 165 ft (50 m).

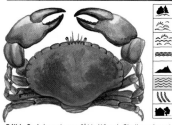

Edible Crab *Length* up to 6¼ in (16 cm). *Shell* very broad, almost oblong, smooth. *Habitat* lower shore under stones, in rock crevices, and on sea bottom to depth of 330 ft (100 m).

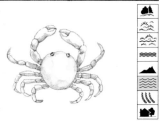

Pea Crab *Length* females up to ½ in (1.5 cm), males half this size. *Shell* transparent with yellow or orange patches; males more greyish yellow. *Habitat* inside mussel shells.

Marbled Crab *Length* up to 2 in (5 cm). *Shell* almost square, varying from green to violet or brown with stripes. *Habitat* upper and lower shore in rock crevices; very fast runner.

Common Hermit Crab *Length* up to 4 in (10 cm). *Shell* almost absent; protects soft-skinned body by living in empty shell of a gastropod, moving to bigger shells as it grows. *Habitat* among rocks on lower shore and shallow water.

Broad-clawed Porcelain Crab *Length* up to ½ in (1.5 cm). *Shell* round and hairy. Walking legs and pincers with hairy edges. *Habitat* among small stones on lower shore and shallow water.

Common Lobster *Length* up to 17¾ in (45 cm). *Colour* blue with orange areas, but turns red when boiled. *Habitat* underwater caves and rock crevices; collected commercially in lobster pots made of wicker.

Dublin Bay Prawn or Scampi *Length* up to 8 in (20 cm), female smaller. *Habitat* soft, sandy bottom at depths of 130-260 ft (40-80 m); collected commercially and eaten throughout Europe. Not a true prawn but a lobster.

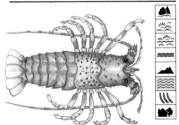

Spiny Lobster or Crawfish *Length* 11¾-20 in (30-50 cm). Unlike Common Lobster has no pincers, but very spiny body which causes deep wounds if stepped on. *Habitat* underwater caves and rock crevices to depth of 230 ft (70 m).

Common Prawn *Length* up to 4¼ in (11 cm). *Colour* semitransparent, pale grey with mauve stripes; turns pink when boiled. *Habitat* lower shore in pools, and in shallow water to depth of 130 ft (40 m).

Common Shrimp *Length* up to 2 in (5 cm). *Colour* semitransparent, grey-brown with red markings; turns pink when boiled. *Habitat* lower shore and shallow water; also found in estuaries where water is saline.

Small Sea Spider *Length* up to ³⁄₅₀ in (1.5 mm), legs ¼ in (6 mm). Will adopt spider-like posture when walking; can swim. *Habitat* among encrusting organisms such as sponges and sea-mats on which they feed by sucking out body juices.

European Oyster *Shell* length up to 4 in (10 cm), very broad, almost circular; surface sculpted into irregular ridges; inner surface smooth pearly white. *Habitat* attached to rocks, in water to depth of 165 ft (50 m); fished commercially.

Common Saddle Oyster *Shell* length up to 2¼ in (6 cm); shell halves unequal, upper domed and heavily sculpted, lower much flatter and c-shaped with hole through which it attaches to rock. *Habitat* lower shore to deep water.

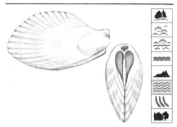

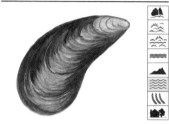

Gaping File Shell *Shell* length up to 1¼ in (3 cm); oblong, asymmetrical, gap between shell halves; thick orange tentacles protrude between shell halves around edge. *Habitat* lower shore and to depth of 330 ft (100 m) among rocks.

Common Mussel *Shell* length up to 4 in (10 cm); shell halves equal, asymmetrical. *Colour* dark blue, black, or brown. *Habitat* attached to rocks and stones by narrow threads on lower shore and shallow water; cultured commercially.

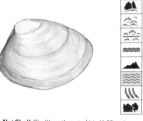

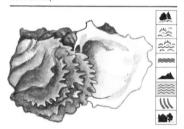

Common Nut Shell *Shell* length up to ½ in (1.25 cm); shell halves equal, triangular, inner margins ridged. *Colour* green to brown. *Habitat* muddy or sandy bottom to depth of 500 ft (150 m).

Mediterranean Jewel Box *Shell* length about 1½ in (4 cm), depth 1½ in (4 cm); shell halves unequal, lower dish-like, attached to surface, upper flatter, like lid; inner surface grooved, purple to brown. *Habitat* on rocks in shallow water.

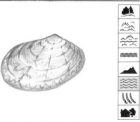

Cross-cut Carpet Shell *Shell* length up to 2¼ in (6 cm); oblong, shell halves equal, surface with concentric rings. *Colour* very variable, patterned green, grey, yellow, or red. *Habitat* burrows in soft mud or sand.

Banded Carpet Shell *Shell* length 2¼ in (6 cm); rounded, shell halves equal, surface with concentric rings. *Colour* variable, brown to red, with radiating pattern of stripes. *Habitat* burrows in soft mud or sand, to depth of 600 ft (180 m).

Brown Venus *Shell* length up to 3¼ in (8 cm); shell halves equal, dome shaped, surface with concentric rings. *Colour* alternating rings of dark and pale brown, with radiating stripes. *Habitat* burrows in soft mud in deep water.

Common Otter Shell *Shell* length up to 4¾ in (12 cm); broad, oblong, shell halves equal, surface with concentric grooves. *Colour* horny outer layer often peels to show paler shell surface. *Habitat* burrows in mud or gravel, to depth of 330 ft (100 m).

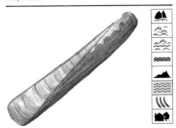

Pod Razor Shell *Shell* length up to 8 in (20 cm); shell halves equal, narrow, rectangular, fragile. *Colour* horny green outer layer peels to show white surface with brown lines. *Habitat* burrows vertically in soft sea bottom or lower shore.

Flask Shell *Shell* length up to 1 in (2.5 cm); shell halves asymmetrical, edges do not meet at front end, surface smooth. *Habitat* lower shore to shallow water; bores into hard sand and soft limestone.

Striped Venus *Shell* length up to 1¾ in (4.5 cm); shell halves similar, with raised concentric rings on surface. *Colour* white, cream, or grey with brown markings. *Habitat* burrows in sand on shore and down to water depth of 180 ft (55 m).

Warty Venus *Shell* length up to 2¼ in (6 cm); shell halves equal, surface concentric rings rough textured. *Colour* white, cream, or grey with brown markings. *Habitat* just below sediment surface to water depth of 330 ft (100 m).

Oval Venus *Shell* length up to ¾ in (2 cm); shell halves equal, surface with radiating ridges. *Colour* fawn to white; inside violet, orange, or white. *Habitat* burrows in sand or gravel in deep water.

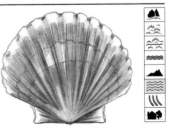

Great Scallop *Shell* length up to 6 in (15 cm); shell halves unequal, lower concave, upper flat with deep ridges forming fan. *Colour* red to brown. *Habitat* on sand and gravel; swim for short distances by forcing water out through valve.

Banded Wedge Shell *Shell* length up to 1½ in (4 cm); shell halves equal, surface finely grooved, inner edge toothed. *Colour* pale brown, yellow, or white with pattern of rays. *Habitat* burrows in sand on lower shore and at depth of 66 ft (20 m).

Hunchback Scallop *Shell* length up to 1½ in (4 cm); shell halves similar, surface with very narrow radiating ribs. *Habitat* attached by fine threads to hard surface, becoming permanently fixed by 'cement' as it ages.

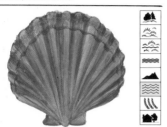

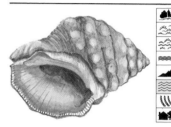

Queen Scallop *Shell* length up to 3½ in (9 cm); shell halves unequal, upper more curved than lower. *Colour* very variable, white, yellow, red, brown, often with spots or stripes. *Habitat* on sand and gravel down to depth of 660 ft (200 m).

Rock Shell *Shell* height about 3¼ in (8 cm); spire thick with rough, knobbly surface; wide shell entrance with toothed margin, orange lip, turning to salmon-pink inside. *Habitat* rock surfaces on lower shore.

Chiton or Coat-of-mail Shell *Shell* length up to 2 in (5 cm), flattened, with 8 central overlapping plates and a middle ridge; tufts of spines around edges. *Colour* grey to yellow. *Habitat* rock surfaces, among weeds, in shallow water.

Common Edible Cockle *Shell* length up to 2 in (5 cm); shell halves equal, outer surface and inner margin finely grooved. *Colour* pale brown to yellow. *Habitat* burrows in sand, lower shore to shallow water; eaten by birds and humans.

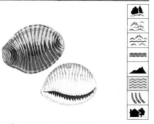

European Cowrie *Shell* height ½ in (1.25 cm); surface sculpted into narrow, transverse ridges; shell opening a lengthwise slit. *Habitat* lower shore to shallow water, on rock surfaces and among sea-squirts.

Violet Sea Snail *Shell* height up to ½ in (1.5 cm), broad, flat whorls with wide shell entrance. *Habitat* floating on sea surface, using air bubbles trapped in web of mucus to give buoyancy; preys on other surface floaters.

Small Limpet *Shell* length up to 1½ in (4 cm), roughly ridged surface. *Colour* variable, grey to pale brown. *Habitat* rock surfaces on the shore.

White Tortoiseshell Limpet *Shell* length up to ½ in (1.2 cm), oval, slightly flattened, with pointed apex. *Colour* cream to pale pink, with pattern of radiating bands. *Habitat* rock surfaces, lower shore to shallow water.

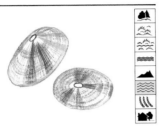

Keyhole Limpet *Shell* length up to 1½ in (4 cm), surface with radiating and fine concentric ridges; hole in apex. *Colour* normally grey, but may be orange, red, or yellow. *Habitat* on rock surfaces, from lower shore down to deep water.

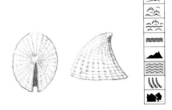

Slit Limpet *Shell* length up to ¾ in (2 cm), surface net-like; narrow slit along side; apex bent to one side. *Colour* variable, grey, white, or pale yellow. *Habitat* surface of boulders on shore, and down to depth of 200 ft (60 m).

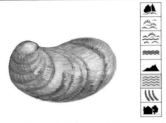

Slipper Limpet *Shell* length up to 2 in (5 cm), roughly oval with small, flat coil at apex; opening half obscured by internal shelf. *Colour* grey, white, brown. *Habitat* on shells or rocks, where often form chains; a pest of Oyster beds.

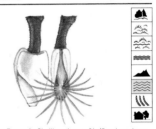

Goose Barnacle *Shell* length up to 2 in (5 cm), made up of 5 thin plates; attached to surface by thick muscular stalk; shell opens to release 12 legs used to trap prey. *Habitat* fixed to slow-moving sailing ships and floating driftwood.

Common Ormer *Shell* length up to 2¾ in (7 cm), flattened, harp shaped, with folded surface and curved line of conspicuous holes. *Colour* brown to olive green; often coated with algae. *Habitat* rock surfaces among weeds in shallow water.

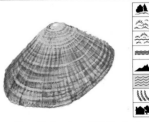

Common Limpet *Shell* length up to 2¾ in (7 cm), outer surface with coarse, radiating ridges, inside very smooth and shiny. *Colour* variable, grey to pale brown; inside translucent orange. *Habitat* rock surfaces, upper to lower shore.

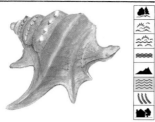 

Pelican's Foot Shell *Shell* height 1¾ in (4.5 cm), spire of nine whorls, each with ring of raised bumps; shell lip with four large spreading points, black to yellow inside. *Habitat* burrows into soft sea bottom, to depth of 265 ft (80 m).

Grooved Top-shell *Shell* height up to ½ in (1 cm), cone-shaped spire, sides almost straight. *Colour* grey or white with red-brown markings. *Habitat* on soft mud and sand, or on seagrass from shore to depth of 330 ft (100 m).

Common Top-shell *Shell* height up to 1¼ in (3 cm), spire broad, cone shaped, straight sided. *Colour* pink or yellow, with wide red-brown stripes; some forms almost white. *Habitat* on rocks and stones from shore to 330 ft (100 m) depth.

Common Dog Whelk *Shell* length up to 2¼ in (6 cm), short, thick spire; shell lips broad, outer lip toothed on margin. *Colour* fawn to cream, often with brown spiral banding. *Habitat* on rock surfaces, from middle shore to shallows.

Small Periwinkle *Shell* height up to ½ in (1 cm), with 5-whorled, sharply pointed spire; smooth, shiny surface. *Colour* brown to blue-black. *Habitat* on rock surfaces and in crevices on upper and middle shore.

Common Wentletrap *Shell* height up to 1½ in (4 cm), narrow, pointed spire with about 10 whorls; projecting ribs resemble cake icing. *Colour* cream, fawn or reddish, some with spiral bands. *Habitat* from shore to 265 ft (80 m), on rocks.

Rough Cockle *Shell* length up to 2¼ in (6 cm); shell halves equal, thick, with deeply sculpted ridges. *Habitat* burrows in sand and silt below water depth of 30 ft (10 m); empty shells frequently washed up by tide.

Purple Heart-urchin *Size* up to 4¾ in (12 cm) long; flattened body covered with short spines; some longer, more prominent spines on upper surface. *Colour* red to purple; empty shell grey with leaf pattern of holes. *Habitat* on sea bottom.

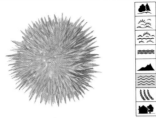

Green Sea-urchin *Size* shell 1⅓ in (3.5 cm) across, spines up to ½ in (1.5 cm) long. *Colour* spines red tipped; empty shell olive green with small mouth opening. *Habitat* among encrusting organisms on which it feeds; down to 1300 ft (400 m).

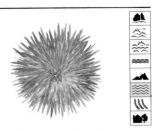

Red Sea-urchin *Size* shell up to 2¼ in (6 cm) across, spines 1¼ in (3 cm) long. *Colour* variable from green to dark brown or red; empty shell pale olive green. *Habitat* rockpools on shore and down to 100 ft (30 m) among seaweed.

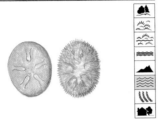

Pea Urchin *Size* shell up to ½ in (1.5 cm) long, spines very short giving felt-like appearance. *Colour* empty shell white with typical pattern of radiating holes. *Habitat* burrows into sand and gravel on lower shore and down to 2600 ft (800 m).

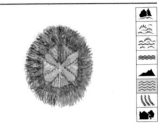

Lyre Urchin *Size* shell up to 2¾ in (7 cm) long, dense felt of short spines. *Colour* red to brown; empty shell pale yellow with characteristic 'lyre' shape below mouth opening. *Habitat* burrows in sand in shallow to deep water.

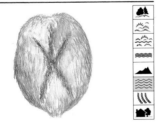

Sea Potato *Size* up to 3½ in (9 cm) long; dense felt of short spines, with few long, curved spines on underside. *Colour* fawn to yellow; empty shell cream coloured. *Habitat* burrows in sand on lower shore and down to 660 ft (200 m).

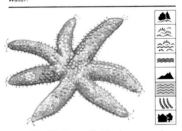

Spotted Starfish *Size* up to 6 in (15 cm) across; number of arms variable from 6-10, and of different lengths. *Colour* fawn, purple, or white, with blue or brown spots. *Habitat* lower shore to depth of 100 ft (30 m), on rocks.

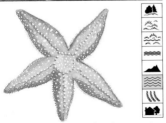

Common Starfish *Size* up to 10 in (25 cm) across; surface covered with short, thick spines. *Colour* pale brown to orange or yellow, underside pale. *Habitat* under rocks and stones on lower shore to shallow water; often washed up by tide.

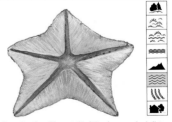

Goosefoot Star *Size* up to 6 in (15 cm) across; body flat, arms barely discernible except for thickened area in midline. *Colour* reddish, pale underside; pattern variable. *Habitat* sandy or muddy bottom from shallow to deep water.

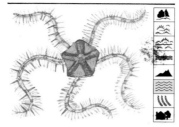

Common Brittle Star *Size* central body disc up to ¾ in (2 cm) across, arms up to 4 in (10 cm); spiny arms often break off but regenerate. *Colour* variable, brown, purple, red, green. *Habitat* under stones in shallow and deep water.

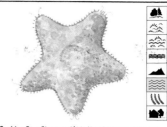

Cushion Star *Size* up to 2¼ in (6 cm) across; rather fat, with short, stubby arms. *Colour* camouflage brown or green with slight pattern; pale underside. *Habitat* under stones and rocks from lower shore to shallow water.

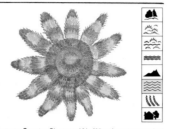

Common Sunstar *Size* up to 10 in (25 cm) across; number of arms variable, from 7-14. *Colour* brown, orange, or red with white patterning. *Habitat* on stony and sandy bottoms, often among the shellfish on which they feed.

Spiny Starfish *Size* up to 31½ in (80 cm) across; surface covered with short spines, each surrounded by a ring of tiny pincers visible with a lens. *Colour* camouflage green-brown, underside yellow. *Habitat* stony bottom down to 600 ft (180 m).

Red Feather Star *Diameter* up to 6 in (15 cm); looks very plant-like with tiny body and long feathery arms. *Colour* dark red to brown. *Habitat* attached to rocks on lower shore and in shallow water by short root-like processes.

Daisy Anemone *Size* up to 1½ in (4 cm) across, height 4 in (10 cm); about 750 tentacles arranged in 9 rings. *Colour* camouflage grey-brown with paler splashes. *Habitat* on rocks and other hard surfaces in shallow water and in rock pools.

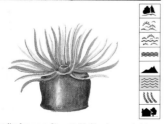

Beadlet Anemone *Size* up to 2 in (5 cm) across, height 2¾ in (7 cm); about 200 tentacles arranged in rings around mouth. *Colour* red, orange-brown, or green, with a ring of blue spots beneath tentacles. *Habitat* on rocks in shallow water.

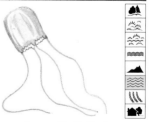

Mediterranean Sea-wasp *Size* 14 in (36 cm) long, with tentacles; umbrella transparent; TENTACLES CONTAIN STINGING CELLS; CONTACT CAN BE VERY PAINFUL. *Habitat* surface of open water and washed up on beaches.

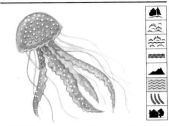

Jellyfish *Size* up to 4 in (10 cm) long; umbrella mushroom shaped with lobed margin and ring of very long tentacles. *Colour* transparent with touches of red or yellow; phosphorescent glow at night. *Habitat* in open water.

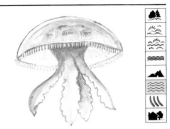

Common Jellyfish *Diameter* up to 10 in (25 cm); transparent, umbrella-shaped mass of jelly with peripheral ring of tiny tentacles; 4 central frilled mouth arms. *Habitat* open water, but commonly washed up on shore.

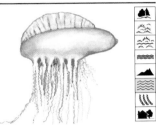

Portuguese Man-of-war *Length* up to 12 in (30 cm), width 4 in (10 cm); upper part with large 'sail', lower part with very long tentacles used for breeding and feeding. DANGEROUS STING, SHOULD NOT BE TOUCHED. *Habitat* open sea surface.

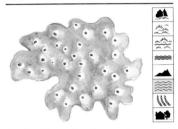

Breadcrumb Sponge Encrusting mass. *Area* up to 10 in (25 cm), height ¾ in (2 cm); surface smooth, with many warty projections containing a central hole. *Colour* green in sunlight, paler in shade. *Habitat* on rocks, lower shore to shallow water.

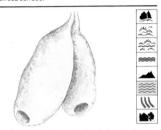

Purse Sponge *Length* up to 2 in (5 cm); dangling, flask-shaped form in water, but become more purse-like when deflated. *Habitat* cluster beneath overhanging rocks and among seaweeds on lower shore and in shallow water.

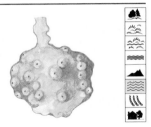

Mermaid's Glove *Size* indeterminate; form either branched or rounded; soft and spongy to the touch as without hard skeleton. *Colour* orange to pink. *Habitat* attached to hard surfaces, subject to strong current effects.

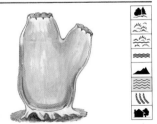

Sea Squirt *Height* up to 4¾ in (12 cm); solitary, tubular individuals with transparent skin and yellow-fringed siphon openings; internal organs visible. *Habitat* shallow water to deep sea bottom, on rocks and wooden surfaces.

Sea Gooseberry *Length* up to 1¼ in (3 cm); a combjelly with 8 lengthways combs and a single pair of tentacles, used for catching plankton. *Habitat* form shoals in coastal waters; swim by beating tiny hairs in combs; luminescent.

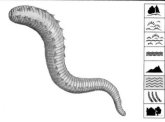

Lugworm *Length* up to 8 in (20 cm); segmented worm thicker at front end, tapering to rear; 13 of segments carry breathing gills for extracting oxygen from water. *Habitat* forms u-shaped burrows in sand of middle to lower shore.

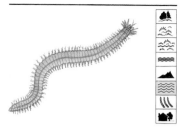

Ragworm *Length* up to 4¾ in (12 cm); each segment has a projection on either side bearing tiny bristles used for movement. *Colour* variable, but usually greenish, with orange or red stripe. *Habitat* burrows in mud on lower shore.

Tube Worm *Length* up to 1¼ in (3 cm); segmented worm with crown of feathery red gill filaments at front end; lies within chalky white cylinder secreted by body, with gills protruding. *Habitat* wooden piers, boat bottoms, and stones.

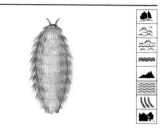

Sea Mouse *Length* up to 6 in (15 cm); segmented worm with segments only visible on hairless underside; upper surface with dense felt of hairs with thick bristles to sides. *Colour* grey with iridescent green sides. *Habitat* mud, sand.

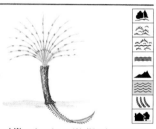

Peacock Worm *Length* up to 10 in (25 cm); segmented worm with 2 fans of narrow gills at head end; in tube made of particles stuck together with mucus; gills withdrawn into tube if disturbed. *Habitat* lower shore and shallow water, in mud.

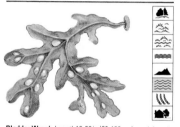

Bladder Wrack *Length* 12-59 in (30-150 cm); each frond ½ in (1.5 cm) wide, thick and rubbery, with numerous air sacs to give buoyancy in the water. *Habitat* attached to rocks between tidelines by small circular holdfast.

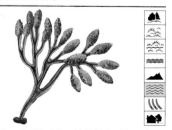

Channelled Wrack *Length* 2-6 in (5-15 cm), fronds ¼ in (6 mm) wide, branched, edges turned in to form channel on one side. *Colour* olive green when wet, but becoming darker as it dries out. *Habitat* attached to rocks between tidelines.

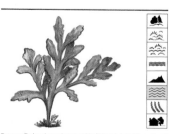

Pepper Dulse *Length* up to 12 in (30 cm), frond broad and flattened. *Colour* variable, from dark red-purple in shady places, to olive green in bright sunlight. *Habitat* attached by root-like holdfast to rocks on shore.

Ballweed *Size* up to 8 in (20 cm) across, frond a round spongy mass made of tangled filaments. *Habitat* attached by root-like holdfast to surface of rocks in shallow water; often washed up on the shore.

Common Coralweed *Length* up to 4¾ in (12 cm), fronds branched, fern-like, with segmented appearance. *Colour* purple, red, pink; when plant dies, chalky white outer skeleton remains. *Habitat* rocks in pools and on lower shore.

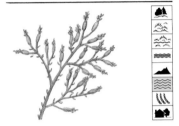

Rainbow Bladderweed *Length* 12-17 in (30-45 cm), branched, bushy fronds, short spines on stem and air sacs at tips. *Colour* olive green, but changes to iridescent blue-green in water. *Habitat* attached to rocks in shallow water.

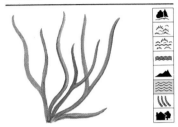

Sea Worms *Length* up to 10 in (25 cm), fronds thick, rubbery and worm-like. *Habitat* attached by tiny round holdfast to rocks on the shore and in shallow water.

Peacock's Tail *Length* up to 4 in (10 cm), hairy frond flat when small but curves inwards to form funnel shape as it enlarges. *Colour* inner surface green to olive or grey. *Habitat* in shallow water, attached to rocks by slender stalk.

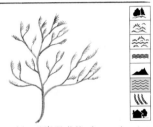

Cockscomb *Length* 3¼-8 in (8-20 cm), narrow branches with tooth-like divisions at tips forming 'combs'. *Habitat* attached by tiny holdfast to surfaces of rocks and stones in shallow water and rock pools; often washed up by tide.

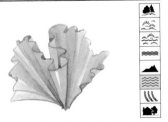

Sea Lettuce *Length* 6-17½ in (15-45 cm), fronds thin, translucent, with irregular shape and wavy margin. *Colour* pale, delicate green, but becoming darker with age. *Habitat* attached by short stalk to rocks in pools and shallow water.

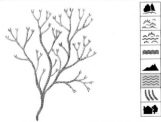

Common Red Ceramium *Length* 3¼-12 in (8-30 cm), fronds narrow and much branched, tips having pincer-like appearance. *Colour* variable, red to brown or yellow, depending on light available. *Habitat* shallow water, on rocks, shells.

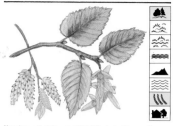

Hornbeam *Height* up to 100 ft (30 m); deciduous. *Flowers* April/May; feathery catkins, female shorter; fruit, a 3-winged nutlet. *Habitat* woodland, often planted to form hedging and to provide very hard timber.

White Willow *Height* up to 80 ft (25 m), spreading habit. *Flowers* April/May; male and female catkins on separate trees. *Habitat* by streams and rivers; pliant twigs used in basket making; wood of one variety used to make cricket bats.

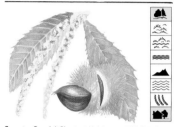

Sweet or Spanish Chestnut *Height* up to 100 ft (30 m); spreading habit. *Flowers* July; yellowish catkins with strong scent; fruit 2 or 3 shiny brown edible nuts in a spiny husk. *Habitat* woodland, in dry soils, often planted in parks.

Walnut *Height* up to 100 ft (30 m); spreading habit, deciduous. *Flowers* April/May; female flower upright green spike, male flowers in catkin; fruit, a hard brown nut in furry green skin. *Habitat* mainly cultivated.

Beech *Height* up to 100 ft (30 m); spreading habit, deciduous. *Flowers* April/May; female flower upright on stiff stalk, male flowers in yellow tassel; fruit, 2 soft-skinned nuts in hairy husk. *Habitat* a forest tree, often grown for timber.

Yew *Height* up to 65 ft (20 m); shrub or small tree, evergreen. *Height* February-April; tiny, green flowers, male and female on different trees; fruit shiny green seed in red fleshy cup, POISONOUS. *Habitat* woodland, scrub, cemeteries.

Juniper *Height* up to 20 ft (6 m); dense, prickly shrub or small tree. *Flowers* March-May; oil of Juniper extracted from green fruits and used to flavour gin; ripe fruits blue-black. *Habitat* forms thickets on dry chalk hills.

Holly *Height* up to 33 ft (10 m); evergreen shrub; leaves very variable but usually with spiny edges. *Flowers* May-August; male and female flower clusters on different plants; RED BERRIES POISONOUS. *Habitat* woods, scrub, hedges, parks.

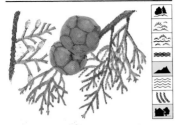

Italian or Funeral Cypress *Height* up to 165 ft (50 m), columnar *Cones* April; tiny, globular. *Habitat* dry hillsides, but the more pyramidal form is commonly planted as an ornamental in gardens and cemeteries.

Silver Fir *Height* up to 230 ft (70 m), pyramidal, with silver-grey bark. *Cones* April/May; upright, long, blunt ended. *Habitat* mainly in higher mountainous regions.

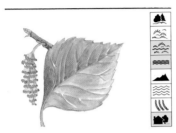

Black Poplar *Height* up to 100 ft (30 m), spreading habit; very dark bark. *Flowers* March/April before leaves appear. *Habitat* by water and damp areas. Many varieties, including Lombardy Poplar from Italy planted as ornamental.

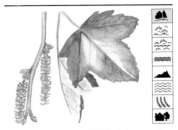

White Poplar *Height* up to 100 ft (30 m), shape roughly triangular; pale smooth bark in young trees. *Flowers* March/April. *Habitat* in damp woodland, and planted as an ornamental. Medicinal preparation made from the leaves.

Oriental Plane *Height* up to 100 ft (30 m), grey bark flakes off to show pale patches. *Flowers* May/June; male and female flowers in separate clusters; fruits chains of spiky balls. *Habitat* in hill regions and as ornamental.

Pedunculate Oak *Height* up to 150 ft (45 m), spreading habit. *Flowers* April/May; chains of yellowish flowers; acorn fruit. *Habitat* mainly on lime-rich soils, in woods, or solitary in hedges; can live to 1000 years; valuable hardwood.

Greater Plantain *Height* 2-12 in (5-30 cm); perennial; broad, oval leaves usually hairless, with prominent stringy veins. *Flowers* June-October: spike of inconspicuous green flowers, purple anthers. *Habitat* waste ground, paths.

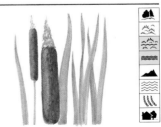

Bulrush or Reedmace *Height* 40-100 in (100-250 cm). *Flowers* June-July; upper part of spike male, lower sausage-shaped section, female, becoming brown as it ripens. *Habitat* beside still or slow-moving streams and ponds.

FLOWERING PLANTS (GREEN/WHITE)

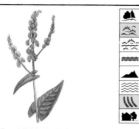

Common Sorrel *Height* 12-40 in (30-100 cm); perennial. *Flowers* May-August; flowers inconspicuous; loose clusters of distinctive red-tinged fruits. *Habitat* grassy places, wasteland; leaves edible, used for salad greens.

Hare's-tail Grass *Height* 2-20 in (5-50 cm); annual. *Flowers* April-June; inconspicuous flowers in oval silky head which persists when dry; often used natural or dyed in flower arrangements. *Habitat* dry coastal hills.

Glasswort *Height* 2-12 in (5-30 cm), fleshy annual with segmented appearance and tiny scale-like leaves pressed close to stem; edible. *Flowers* August-September; tiny inconspicuous petals. *Habitat* saltmarshes, mudflats.

Petty Spurge *Height* 4-12 in (10-30 cm); annual. *Flowers* April-November; tiny flowers with green petals form flat cluster at top of stem. *Habitat* bare, disturbed ground in fields, gardens, by roadsides.

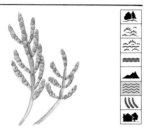

Marsh Cudweed *Height* 4-8 in (10-20 cm); annual with silvery grey leaves, much-branched stem. *Flowers* July-October; bud-like, without outer petals. *Habitat* damp bare places, stream and river banks.

Lady's Mantle *Height* 4-12 in (10-30 cm); perennial with softly hairy lobed leaves. *Height* May-September; tiny petal-less flowers surrounded by green calyx; loose terminal clusters. *Habitat* grassy places, woodland edge, rocks.

Hairy Bitter-cress *Height* 2-8 in (5-20 cm); annual with basal rosette of divided hairy leaves. *Flowers* March-October; tiny flowers less than 1/4 in (5 mm) across; seeds in long erect pods. *Habitat* bare ground, fields, paths, gardens.

Shepherd's Purse *Height* 2-24 in (5-60 cm); annual. *Flowers* throughout year; tiny flowers 1/10 in (2-3 mm) across; seed capsule distinctive heart or purse shape. *Habitat* any bare, disturbed, or cultivated ground.

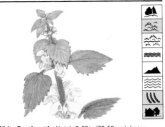

White Dead-nettle *Height* 8-20 in (20-50 cm); hairy perennial, spreading by underground roots to form clumps. *Flowers* March-November. *Habitat* roadsides, waste places, cultivated ground.

Alpine Anemone *Height* 6-12 in (15-30 cm); perennial; much divided, ferny leaves. *Flowers* May-July; stems carrying large solitary flower, white or yellow; seeds with feathery plume. *Habitat* mountain meadows; up to 9500 ft (2900 m).

Solomon's Seal *Height* 12-22½ in (30-70 cm); drooping hairless perennial. *Flowers* May-June; berries dark blue, poisonous. *Habitat* damp woodland, cultivated in gardens. Powdered root used for medicinal purposes.

White-star-of-Bethlehem *Height* 4-12 in (10-30 cm); bulb perennial with grass-like leaves. *Flowers* April-May. *Habitat* grassy places, vineyards, roadsides.

Garlic Mustard *Height* 8-40 in (20-100 cm); biennial; wrinkled, heart-shaped leaves give off strong smell of garlic when crushed. *Flowers* April-August; seeds in long pods. *Habitat* hedges, woodland edge, by shaded paths.

Corn Chamomile *Height* 4-20 in (10-50 cm); annual with much-divided feathery greyish leaves. *Flowers* May-October. *Habitat* on chalky soils, cornfields, besides paths, waste ground.

Scentless Mayweed *Height* 4-20 in (10-50 cm); annual; feathery green leaves without aromatic scent of similar plants. *Flowers* April-October. *Habitat* cultivated land, waste ground.

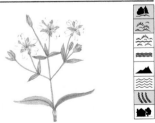

Greater Stitchwort *Height* 4-12 in (10-30 cm); perennial; erect strap-shaped leaves, smooth on upper surface. *Flowers* April-June; flower width ¾-1¼ in (20-30 mm); deeply notched petals. *Habitat* woodland edge, hedges, scrub.

FLOWERING PLANTS (WHITE)

Wood Sorrel *Height* 2-4¾ in (5-12 cm); soft, creeping perennial; leaves close up at night. *Flowers* April-May; delicate, usually white, occasionally pale pink or blue. *Habitat* deciduous woodland and mountainsides.

Hogweed *Height* 32-60 in (80-150 cm); biennial or perennial; stout hollow stem ridged and bristly. *Flowers* April-November; in broad flat clusters up to 8 in (20 cm) across, white to pale pink. *Habitat* meadows, damp woods, paths.

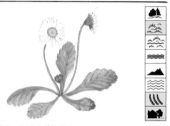

Daisy *Height* 2-3¼ in (5-8 cm) when flowering; hairy perennial, forming flat rosette of leaves. *Flowers* throughout year; flowers carried on flexible leafless stalks. *Habitat* in short grass, lawns, meadows.

Ox-eye Daisy *Height* 8-20 in (20-50 cm); coarse-leaved perennial. *Flowers* May-September; up to 2 in (5 cm) across. *Habitat* grassy places, waste ground, roadside verges.

Traveller's Joy or Old Man's Beard *Length* 10-26 ft (3-8 m); woody climbing perennial. *Flowers* June-September; seeds in clusters with long white feathery plumes. *Habitat* scrambling in hedges, woodland edge.

Great Bindweed *Length* 40-120 in (1-3 m); twining perennial with smooth heart-shaped leaves. *Flowers* June-September; up to 3 in (75 mm) across, set in large fleshy bracts. *Habitat* in hedges, waste ground, gardens.

Field Rose *Height* up to 40 in (1 m); clambering woody shrub with curved thorns on stem. *Flowers* July-August; always white, unlike similar pink or white Dog Rose; fruits, red hips. *Habitat* hedges, woodland edge.

Watercress *Height* 12-32 in (30-80 cm); upright or creeping perennial with hollow stem and smooth, lobed leaves; edible. *Flowers* May-October. *Habitat* in shallow, fast-moving water, streams, ditches.

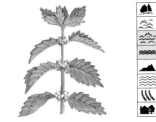

Gypsywort *Height* 8-32 in (20-80 cm); perennial with nettle-like leaves. *Flowers* July-September; tiny white flowers arranged in compact whorls in leaf axils. *Habitat* damp places, ditches, marshes, river banks.

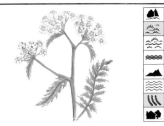

Yarrow *Height* 6-20 in (15-50 cm); perennial; feathery aromatic leaves with greyish downy hair. *Flowers* June-November; in flat-topped clusters, white or pale pink. *Habitat* grassy fields, hedgerows, roadsides.

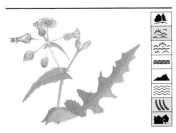

Common Sowthistle *Height* 8-40 in (20-100 cm); annual; leaves very smooth. *Flowers* May-November; flowers in loose clusters; seeds in a 'clock'. *Habitat* field edges, gardens, waste ground.

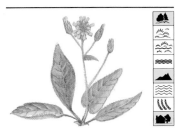

Rock or Few-leaved Hawkweed *Height* 8-24 in (20-60 cm); stem usually leafless. *Flowers* June-August. *Habitat* rocky places, walls, and deciduous woodland; in mountain regions up to 6600 ft (2000 m).

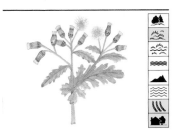

Groundsel *Height* 4-12 in (10-30 cm); sticky, smooth-leaved annual. *Flowers* February-November; bud-like, without long petals; seeds with parachute of hairs. *Habitat* any bare, disturbed ground, fields, roadsides.

Common Ragwort *Height* 12-24 in (30-60 cm); biennial; leaves blunt tipped. *Flowers* June-November. *Habitat* grassy fields and meadows. Poisonous to cattle.

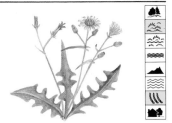

Smooth Hawksbeard *Height* 12-24 in (30-60 cm); perennial; upper leaf surface hairless. *Flowers* June-November; flowers in loose clusters; seeds ribbed, arranged in a 'clock'. *Habitat* grassy places, fields.

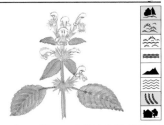

Large-flowered Hemp-nettle *Height* 12-32 in (30-80 cm); hairy annual. *Flowers* July-September; flowers with purple lower lip. *Habitat* woodland clearings, fields, wasteland, cultivated land.

Creeping Buttercup *Length* 4-16 in (10-40 cm) perennial; spreads by runners. *Flowers* May-September; distinguished from similar Meadow Buttercup by stalked terminal leaf lobe. *Habitat* damp meadows, riverbanks.

Globe Flower *Height* 12-24 in (30-60 cm); perennial. *Flowers* May-July; flowers rounded, up to 2 in (5 cm) across; sepals yellow, curving in around true, petal-less flower. *Habitat* damp grassy meadows up to 8000 ft (2400 m).

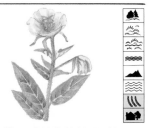

Evening Primrose *Height* 20-47 in (50-120 cm), biennial with deep taproot. *Flowers* June-September; sweetly scented, often opening at dusk. *Habitat* bare ground, roadsides; naturalized garden escape from USA.

Henbane *Height* 12-24 in (30-60 cm); annual. *Flowers* May-September; dry brown seeds in a capsule. *Habitat* bare places, mainly by the sea, also disturbed ground inland occasionally. ALL PARTS POISONOUS, CAN BE FATAL IF EATEN.

Bird's-foot Trefoil *Height* 2-12 in (5-30 cm); low sprawling perennial. *Flowers* May-September; yellow to orange or red; long seedpods arranged like a bird's foot. *Habitat* grassy fields and meadows.

Silverweed *Length* up to 32 in (80 cm); low creeping perennial, spreading by runners; leaves with silvery down, especially on underside. *Flowers* May-August. *Habitat* grassy areas by roads, paths, rivers.

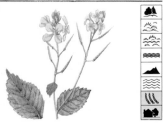

Charlock *Height* 12-24 in (30-60 cm); annual with roughly hairy stem and leaves. *Flowers* April-October; flowers ½-¾ in (15-20 mm) across; seeds in very nodular pod. *Habitat* preferably on lime soils, cultivated and waste land.

Wild Cabbage *Height* 12-24 in (30-60 cm); perennial; older plants with thick, woody stem. *Flowers* May-September; in long spike. *Habitat* on sea cliffs, also garden escape by roadside, cultivated as cauliflower and cabbage.

Yellow-star-of-Bethlehem *Height* 4-12 in (10-30 cm); bulb plant. *Flowers* April-May. *Habitat* damp, deciduous woodland, grassy fields, and meadows; in mountains up to 5600 ft (1700 m).

Common or Perforate St John's Wort *Height* 12-24 in (30-60 cm); perennial; separated from similar plants by 2 prominent ridges at sides of stem. *Flowers* July-September; flowers deep yellow with black dots. *Habitat* woodland edge, scrub.

Yellow Loosestrife *Height* 20-48 in (50-120 cm); perennial; oval leaves with tiny black dots. *Flowers* July-August; up to ¾ in (2 cm) across, arranged in loose clusters. *Habitat* wet places, ditches, fens, river banks.

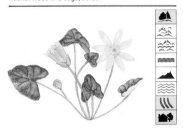

Lesser Celandine *Height* 2-6 in (5-15 cm); perennial with fleshy stem and shiny heart-shaped leaves. *Flowers* March-May; up to 1¼ in (3 cm) across, petals shining. *Habitat* damp woodland, hedgerows, gardens.

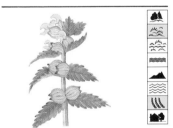

Yellow Rattle *Height* 6-16 in (15-40 cm); semiparasitic annual *Flowers* May-September; set in conspicuous rounded bracts; seeds rattle inside capsule when ripe. *Habitat* grassy meadows, cultivated fields.

Common Rock-rose *Height* 4-12 in (10-30 cm); erect or sprawling perennial with woody stems. *Flowers* May-September; colour white, pink, orange, usually yellow. *Habitat* dry chalk grassland, rocky places; up to 9275 ft (2820 m).

Great Yellow Gentian *Height* 16-55 in (40-140 cm); perennial with fleshy root used to flavour aperitifs taken as tonic. *Flowers* June-August; flowers set in boat-shaped bracts. *Habitat* grassy mountain slopes up to 8225 ft (2500 m).

Primrose *Height* up to 4¾ in (12 cm); perennial, soft, hairy leaves forming ring at base of flower stalk. *Flowers* ¾-1¼ in (20-30 mm) across. *Habitat* forms irregular patches in deciduous woodland, grassy banks, hedgerows.

FLOWERING PLANTS (YELLOW/PINK)

Great Leopard's-bane *Height* 8-20 in (20-50 cm); upright, hairy perennial, spreading by underground stems. *Flowers* May-July; 1½-2½ in (40-60 mm) across, in clusters. *Habitat* woodland, shady places, in mountain areas.

Great Mullein *Height* 8-80 in (20-200 cm); biennial; leaves up to 16 in (40 cm) long, covered with thick grey down. *Flowers* June-August. *Habitat* dry woodland clearings, grassy places. Once used as torches by coating plant with tallow.

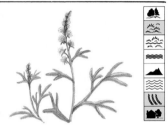

Wild Mignionette *Height* 8-20 in (20-50 cm); perennial; distinguished from similar Weld by toothed leaves and sweet scent. *Flowers* June-September, in tall spike. *Habitat* bare, disturbed ground, quarries, wasteland.

Common Cow-wheat *Height* 4-20 in (10-50 cm); semiparasitic annual. *Flowers* May-September, either pale yellow or white with pink tinge. *Habitat* woodland edge, moorland, heaths.

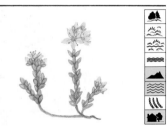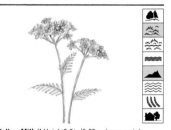

Biting Stonecrop *Height* 2-6 in (5-15 cm) perennial forming dense, fleshy leaved mat. *Flowers* May-July; flowers ½ in (12 mm) across, at tips of branching stems. *Habitat* dry, stony places, walls, roofs, shingle, rocky cliffs.

Yellow Milfoil *Height* 2-8 in (5-20 cm); perennial; narrow feathery leaves, covered with silvery down. *Flowers* May-July. *Habitat* poor dry grassland, rocky slopes, in mountain areas.

Gorse *Height* up to 10 ft (2.5 m); evergreen shrub, densely spiny. *Flowers* throughout year; seeds in hairy pod up to ¾ in (20 mm). *Habitat* sandy soils, heathland, woodland edge.

Butterbur *Height* 4-16 in (10-40 cm) when flowering; perennial, forming dense patches; leaves up to 40 in (1 m) wide, downy hairs on underside. *Flowers* March-May, before leaves; male and female on different plants. *Habitat* riverbanks.

Herb Robert *Height* 8-20 in (20-50 cm); annual. *Flowers* April-November; fruits with long 'beak'. *Habitat* shady banks, hedges, on shingle beaches; distinguished from similar pink Crane's-bill by hairy stem, reddish leaves.

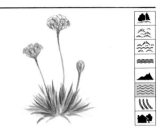

Sea Pink or Thrift *Height* 2-12 in (5-30 cm); perennial; formes dense-green cushions of narrow leaves. *Flowers* April-August; in round heads up to 1¼ in (3 cm) across. *Habitat* coastal areas, on cliffs, sand-dunes.

Red Dead-nettle *Height* 4-12 in (10-30 cm); annual; soft, hairy leaves. *Flowers* March-September. *Habitat* waste land, woodland edge, cultivated ground.

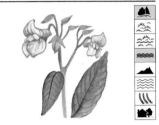

Himalayan Balsam *Height* 20-80 in (50-200 cm); *Flowers* July-October; colour white, pink, or purple; seed capsules break open explosively if touched. *Habitat* along river banks, wet woods; originally from Himalayas, naturalized.

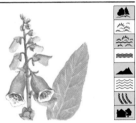

Foxglove *Height* up to 60 in (1.5 m); biennial. *Flowers* June-September; usually purple, rarely white. *Habitat* woodland clearings, hedgerows, wet mountain slopes; often cultivated; source of heart-stimulant drug.

Lesser Burdock *Height* 24-48 in (60-120 cm); tough, hairy biennial. *Flowers* July-September; flowers set in rounded heads with hooked spines which dry to form sticky burs. *Habitat* waste ground, shaded areas.

Creeping Thistle *Height* 24-48 in (60-120 cm); deep-rooted perennial with smooth stem and spiny leaf margins. *Flowers* June-September; heads up to 1¼ in (3 cm) across; seeds carried by feathery down. *Habitat* cultivated and waste ground.

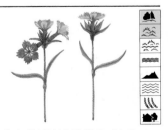

Carthusian Pink *Height* 6-16 in (15-40 cm); hairless perennial with strap-shaped leaves. *Flowers* May-August; colour dark pink or red, set in brown bracts. *Habitat* grassland on chalky soil, woodland edge.

Wild Thyme *Height* 2-6 in (5-15 cm); hairy stemmed shrub with creeping, horizontal branches; aromatic leaves. *Flowers* June-September; colour pale pink to purple. *Habitat* dry grassland, open woods, up to 10 000 ft (3000 m).

Common Mallow *Height* 16-48 in (40-120 cm); annual with large, broad leaves, 3¼-4 in (8-10 cm). *Flowers* June-October; colour pale pink to purple, petals with deeply indented margin. *Habitat* dry soils by roadside, waste ground.

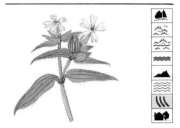

Night-flowering Catchfly *Height* 12-24 in (30-60 cm); hairy annual. *Flowers* July-August; pink petals with yellow underside, open at night, very fragrant. *Habitat* dry, cultivated land, beside paths.

Field Bindweed *Height* up to 80 in (2 m); creeping perennial which twists around other plants and solid supports. *Flowers* June-September; colour usually pink, occasionally white. *Habitat* fields, hedges, gardens.

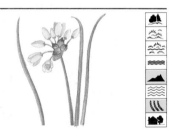

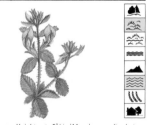

Rose Garlic *Height* 6-16 in (15-40 cm); bulb perennial with grass-like leaves, smelling strongly of garlic. *Flowers* April-June; pale-pink flowers in rounded cluster. *Habitat* rocky hillsides, rough fields.

Restharrow *Height* up to 5½ in (14 cm); sprawling hairy perennial with occasional spines. *Flowers* July-September; in short spikes; colour pink to purple. *Habitat* sandy soil by coast, chalky soil inland, grassy places.

Water Avens *Height* 8-80 in (20-100 cm); softly hairy perennial. *Flowers* April-September; nodding on curved stems, sepals purple-red; hooked, hairy seeds. *Habitat* damp, shady places, woods, river banks; up to 6600 ft (2000 m).

Soapwort *Height* 12-32 in (30-80 cm); smooth-leaved perennial. *Flowers* June-September; colour pink to white. *Habitat* damp fields, hedgerows, river banks, roadsides. Can be boiled to produce a soapy washing liquid.

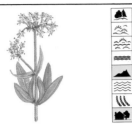

Red Valerian *Height* 12-32 in (30-80 cm), smooth-stemmed fleshy perennial with blue-green leaves. *Flowers* March-September; colour pink or white; *Habitat* rocky cliffs, old walls; often cultivated as ornamental.

Rosebay Willowherb *Height* 20-60 in (50-150 cm), perennial; hairless stem and leaves, reddish in dry situations. *Flowers* July-September. *Habitat* often colonizes burnt ground, also on walls, waste ground, and woodland clearings.

Scarlet Pimpernel *Length* up to 8 in (20 cm); prostrate annual with smooth oval leaves. *Flowers* May-October; colour usually red, but also pink or blue; seeds in round capsule. *Habitat* cultivated fields, sand-dunes.

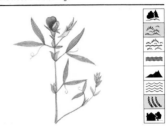

Red Vetchling *Length* up to 24 in (60 cm); hairless sprawling annual with very narrow leaves. *Flowers* March-May; large single flowers up to ½ in (15 mm) across. *Habitat* rough grassland and cultivated fields.

Red Clover *Height* 4-12 in (10-30 cm); perennial; rather narrow hairy leaves, often with central white crescent. *Flowers* May-October. *Habitat* grassy meadows, roadsides; often cultivated for animal fodder.

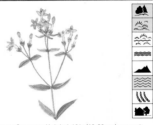

Common Centaury *Height* 4-12 in (10-30 cm); smooth grey-green annual, with leaves in basal rosette. *Flowers* June-September, usually in a terminal cluster. *Habitat* sand-dunes, dry woodland, and grassland near coast.

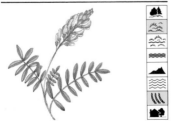

Sanfoin *Height* 12-24 in (30-60 cm); downy upright perennial. *Flowers* June-September; seeds in rough-textured pod. *Habitat* chalk grassland; cultivated for animal fodder.

Cat's-foot or Mountain Everlasting *Height* 2-8 in (5-20 cm); perennial; leaves covered with thick white down on underside. *Flowers* June-July; petal-like bracts pink or white. *Habitat* grassy mountain slopes.

Common Poppy *Height* 8-32 in (20-80 cm); hairy annual; solitary or in dense carpet. *Flowers* 2¾-4 in (7-10 cm) across; April-July; tiny seeds in 'pepperpot' capsule. *Habitat* cornfields, roadsides, gardens.

Redshank *Height* 4-12 in (10-30 cm); sprawling, hairless annual usually with dark central blotch on leaves. *Flowers* June-October; colour pale pink to white. *Habitat* waste ground and near streams, rivers.

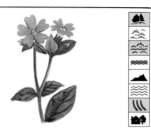

Red Campion *Height* 12-32 in (30-80 cm); softly hairy perennial with oval leaves. *Flowers* March-November; colour red or pink. *Habitat* damp shady places, woodland edge, hedges, roadside verges.

Distaff Thistle *Height* up to 10 in (25 cm); annual leaves covered with white down, long bristly hairs around the edges. *Flowers* April-July; small flower heads surrounded by curved spiny bracts. *Habitat* dry hillsides, paths.

Marsh Woundwort *Height* 12-40 in (30-100 cm); perennial with roughly hairy wrinkled leaves. *Flowers* June-September. *Habitat* damp places, beside ponds and rivers, damp fields.

Sea Lavender *Height* 8-20 in (20-50 cm); perennial; much-branched stems. *Flowers* July-September; dead, dried flowers persist. *Habitat* form dense patches in saltmarshes around Atlantic coast.

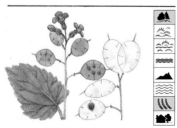

Honesty *Height* 12-48 in (30-120 cm); biennial. *Flowers* April-June; several colour forms; often garden escapes; seeds in rounded, transparent capsules which persist when dry. *Habitat* hedgerows, damp woods.

Opium Poppy *Height* 16-40 in (40-100 cm); annual; large, smooth greyish leaves. *Flowers* April-July; usually lilac or red; petal number and shape variable. *Habitat* bare disturbed ground. Opium not present in temperate areas.

Comfrey *Height* 12-40 in (30-100 cm); perennial; leaves with stiff hairs which can irritate the skin. *Flowers* May-June; white or purple. *Habitat* riverbanks, wet meadows, damp woodland; medicinal herb.

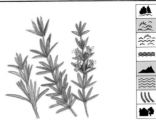

Rosemary *Height* up to 60 in (1.5 m); woody shrub with narrow aromatic leaves used as culinary herb. *Flowers* throughout year. *Habitat* on dry coastal hills, often in dense thickets. Rosemary Oil used in perfume industry.

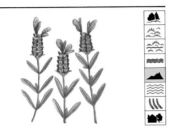

French Lavender *Height* 12-24 in (30-60 cm); woody aromatic shrub with narrow silvery leaves; used to deter moths and perfume linen. *Flowers* February-June; conspicuous purple bracts above flower heads. *Habitat* dry hills.

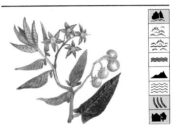

Woody Nightshade or Bittersweet *Length* 20-60 in (50-150 cm); trailing woody perennial. *Flowers* May-September; oval fruits becoming red as they ripen, POISONOUS. Other nightshades black fruits. *Habitat* woodland, hedges, waste ground.

Ivy-leaved Toadflax *Length* 12-24 in (30-60 cm); smooth-leaved trailing perennial. *Flowers* April-November. *Habitat* originally a mountain plant, but commonly found scrambling over walls and bare, stony places.

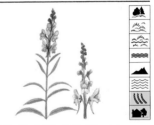

Purple Toadflax *Height* up to 47 in (120 cm) when flowering; perennial. *Flowers* June-August in long slender spikes. *Habitat* bare ground, gardens, on walls.

Tufted Vetch *Length* up to 40 in (1 m); prostrate perennial scrambling up other plants using tendrils. *Flowers* June-August; arranged to one side of long-stalked spike. *Habitat* grassy meadows, hedge banks; up to 7250 ft (2200 m).

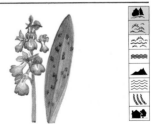

Early Purple Orchid *Height* 6-16 in (15-40 cm); perennial; leaves commonly with dark spots, but also unspotted. *Flowers* April-June; unpleasant cat urine smell. *Habitat* in open woodland and chalky downland.

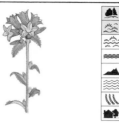

Clustered Bellflower *Height* 8-24 in (20-60 cm); perennial; lower leaves heart shaped, stalked, upper leaves narrow, unstalked. *Flowers* June-October; most flowers in dense terminal cluster. *Habitat* chalk grassland, woods.

Self-heal *Height* 4-8 in (10-20 cm); hairy creeping perennial spreading by runners. *Flowers* June-November; colour purple, occasionally pink or white. *Habitat* cultivated land, grassy fields, woodland clearings.

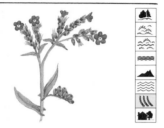

True Alkanet *Height* 12-32 in (30-80 cm); hairy biennial. *Flowers* June-August; purple flowers up to ½ in (15 mm) across, in drooping cluster. *Habitat* dry cultivated fields, hedge banks, grassy paths. Root is source of red dye.

Dame's Violet *Height* 16-40 in (40-100 cm); perennial; leaves roughly hairy. *Flowers* May-August; white, violet, or lilac, sweetly scented; seeds in upright pods. *Habitat* damp places, hedgerows, garden escape.

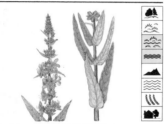

Purple Loosestrife *Height* 20-60 in (50-120 cm); perennial. *Flowers* June-September; arranged in whorls around stem forming tall purple spike. *Habitat* in wet places, ditches, river banks, beside ponds.

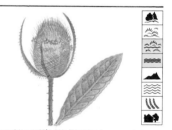

Teasel *Height* 27½-60 in (70-150 cm); perennial, stem very prickly. *Flowers* July-August, flowers set into green spiky head which dries and persists; head once used as brush in cloth making. *Habitat* river banks, damp ditches.

Ground Ivy *Height* 8-16 in (20-40 cm); hairy, sprawling perennial. *Flowers* March-June. *Habitat* common weed of cultivation, also woods and hedges; ancient ale herb used to flavour beer before introduction of hops.

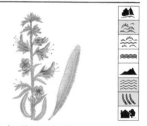

Viper's Bugloss *Height* 12-24 in (30-60 cm); stiff bristly perennial. *Flowers* May-August; buds pink, opening to blue. *Habitat* dry open places, quarries, stony fields, beside paths, sand-dunes.

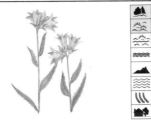

Rampion Bell-flower *Height* 20-32 in (50-80 cm);
biennial with slender stem and narrow hairy leaves.
Flowers May-August. *Habitat* dry fields, woodland
edge, scrub.

Borage *Height* 8-24 in (20-60 cm); annual; leaves and
stem bristly. *Flowers* May-September. *Habitat*
roadsides, vineyards; often cultivated as medicinal
herb to lower fevers and relieve coughs.

Chicory *Height* 12-48 in (30-120 cm); stiff hairy perennial
with narrow upright leaves. *Flowers* May-September;
usually blue, occasionally pink or white. *Habitat*
roadsides, waste ground. Leaves and roots eaten.

Common or Field Forget-me-not *Height* 4-17 in (10-
40 cm); hairy annual or biennial. *Flowers* April-October,
each flower ¹⁄₁₀-¹⁄₅ in (3-5 mm) across. *Habitat* dry, bare
ground in cultivated fields, roadsides, gardens.

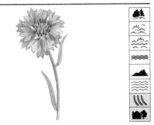

Cornflower *Height* 12-32 in (30-80 cm); annual; narrow
leaves and stem with white downy covering. *Flowers*
June-August; up to 1¼ in (3 cm) across. *Habitat* waste
ground, field margins, increasingly uncommon in
cornfields.

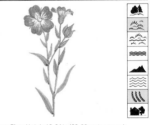

Common Flax *Height* 12-24 in (30-60 cm); annual;
slender stem and narrow upright leaves. *Flowers* June-
October. *Habitat* meadows; often cultivated to provide
linen threads from stem, and linseed oil from seeds.

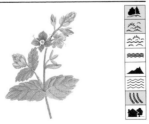

Germander Speedwell *Height* 4-12 in (10-30 cm);
annual. *Flowers* April-June; flowers much brighter blue
than similar Field Speedwell. *Habitat* damp woods,
hedges, grassy places, gardens.

Bugle *Height* up to 6 in (15 cm); creeping perennial
spreading by runners; leaves and stem often reddish.
Flowers April-June; colour blue, occasionally pink or
white. *Habitat* damp grassland, paths, woodland
clearings.

We have kept technical terms to a minimum, but a few are unavoidable and are defined here. A very few are also defined in the text, but are repeated here for ease of reference. Words used in a definition which are themselves defined in this glossary are printed in small capitals.

annual any flowering plant that completes its life cycle and then dies within a single growing season.

antenna one of a pair of sense organs or 'feelers' on the head of an insect, millipede, or centipede, richly endowed with scent and touch detectors.

anther the male, pollen-producing structures of a flower.

aromatic of plants which secrete scented oils that evaporate readily; includes most culinary herbs.

axil the upper angle between a small stem or branch and a larger one, or where a leaf stalk joins a stem.

biennial a flowering plant that takes two years to complete its life cycle and die; typically, food is stored in the first year, and flowering and seed production occur in the second year.

bocage a landscape pattern typical of northern France, comprising a network of hedgerows and woodland clumps, enclosing small fields.

bract a leaf, usually small or modified, which grows in the AXIL of a flower or INFLORESCENCE.

calcareous rock a rock, such as chalk or limestone, often formed from the laying down and compression of vast millions of skeletons of prehistoric microscopic marine creatures, largely composed of calcium carbonate.

capsule a dry fruit which splits open to release seeds.

climax vegetation the final, self-perpetuating stage in a succession through time of plant communities which have reached a balance with the environment.

crystalline rock rock which has been formed by crystallization from a liquid, molten state or under great pressure.

deciduous of trees which shed their leaves seasonally, usually autumn, and spend at least part of the year in a leafless state.

elytron(a) the horny wing case of earwigs, beetles, and some bugs, formed of modified forewings and which protect the hindwings when at rest.

endemic of a plant or animal whose geographical distribution is restricted to the region under discussion.

evergreen tree with persistent leaves which are not shed seasonally.

garrigue low-growing vegetation, derived from primary Mediterranean forest and replacing it over much of the region as a result of several millennia of human interference, especially grazing by goats; dwarf, prickly shrubs and aromatic herbs with drought-resistant foliage dominate.

gastropod literally, 'stomach foot', referring to those molluscs, such as snails and slugs, which move along by means of a single, large, mucus-secreting muscular foot on the underside of the body.

inflorescence the particular pattern of arrangement of flowers of a given kind of plant.

invertebrate of animals, such as worms, snails, and insects, which have no vertebrae or backbone.

maquis a dense, evergreen community of shrubs, between 40 and 120 inches (1 and 3 metres) high which develops in Mediterranean areas after forest clearance.

passage migrant of birds which migrate between a wintering area in southern, warm countries and a summer breeding area in northern countries.

perennial a flowering plant which normally lives for two or more growing seasons and flowers annually, perhaps after an initial period of one to several years without flowering.

primitively social of wasps and bees, where there is no clear-cut distinction between an exclusively egg-laying queen and a worker caste, and social organization is poorly developed.

proboscis the tubular sucking mouthparts of many kinds of insect.

scree coarse rock debris that accumulates at the base of an inland cliff, being continually added to by the weathering and fragmentation of the cliff face.

sepal one of the outer floral leaves in a flower.

siphon in sea squirts, a pair of hollow tubes lined with waving microscopic hairs that generate water currents which carry in food particles; in water bugs and the aquatic larvae of some flies, a hollow breathing tube which pierces the surface film of water.

social living together in colonies, as in ants, wasps, and bees.

solitary of wasps and bees, where each female lives alone and builds her own nest, with no co-operation with other individuals.

succulent a plant with swollen, fleshy leaves which are juicy and retain water; succulent structures (stems and/or leaves) are an adaptation for survival in dry conditions.

tap root a large, central root descending into the soil much deeper than the other roots on a plant, an adaptation to reach soil water at depth; often found in plants in well-drained or arid soils.

tendril part of a stem, leaf, or leaf stalk which is modified as a thread-like, twisted climbing structure; found in plants such as sweet peas.

whorl a complete coil of a marine or land snail's shell.

FURTHER READING

General

Harris, T. 1982. *The Natural History of the Mediterranean.* Pelham Books, London.

Polunin, O and Walters, M. 1985. *A Guide to the Vegetation of Britain and Europe.* Oxford University Press, Oxford.

Seashore

Barnes, R. 1979. *The Natural History of Britain and Northern Europe: Coasts and Estuaries.* Hodder and Stoughton, London.

Campbell, A C. 1976. *The Country Life Guide to the Seashore and Shallow Seas of Britain and Europe*. Hamlyn Publishing Group, London.

Campbell, A C. 1982. *The Hamlyn Guide to the Flora and Fauna of the Mediterranean Sea*. Hamlyn Publishing Group, London.

Plants

Fitter, R and Fitter, A. 1984. *Collins Guide to the Grasses, Sedges, Rushes and Ferns of Britain and Northern Europe*. Collins & Co Ltd, London.

Grey-Wilson, C. 1979. *The Alpine Flowers of Britain and Europe*. Collins & Co Ltd, London.

Polunin, O. 1972. *The Concise Flowers of Europe*. Oxford University Press, London.

Polunin, O and Huxley, A. 1981. *Flowers of the Mediterranean*. Chatto and Windus, London.

Reed, J. L 1954. *Forests of France*. Faber and Faber, London.

Schauer, T. 1978. *A Field Guide to the Wild Flowers of Britain and Europe*. Collins & Co Ltd, London.

Invertebrates

d'Aguilar, J, Dommanget, J-L, and Préhac, R. 1986. *A Field Guide to the Dragonflies of Britain, Europe, and North Africa*. Collins & Co Ltd, London.

Chinery, M. 1986. *Collins Field Guide to the Insects of Britain and Western Europe*. Collins & Co Ltd, London.

Harde, K W. 1984. *A Field Guide in Colour to Beetles*. Octopus Books Ltd, London.

Higgins, L G. 1983. *The Butterflies of Britain and Europe*. Collins & Co Ltd, London.

Jones, Dick. 1984. *The Country Life Guide to Spiders of Britain and Northern Europe*. Country Life Books, London.

Kerney, M P and Cameron, R A D. 1979. *A Field Guide to the Land Snails of Britain and North-West Europe*. Collins & Co Ltd, London.

Reptiles and amphibians

Arnold, E N and Burton, J A. 1978. *A Field Guide to the Reptiles and Amphibians of Britain and Europe*. Collins & Co Ltd, London.

Birds

Heinzel, H, Fitter, R, and Parslow, J. 1972. *The Birds of Britain and Europe, with North Africa and the Middle East*. Collins & Co, Ltd, London.

Peterson, R, Mountfort, G and Hollom, P A D. Revised ed. 1983. *A Field Guide to the Birds of Britain and Europe*. Collins & Co Ltd, London.

Mammals

Van Den Brink, F H. 1967. *A Field Guide to the Mammals of Britain and Europe*. Collins & Co Ltd, London.

Corbett, G and Ovenden D. 1980. *The Mammals of Britain and Europe*. Collins & Co Ltd, London.

INDEX